Make Marzipan, not War

Make Marzipan, not War
Crazy rhymes for crazy times

Sabrina P. Ramet

 An imprint of New Academia Publishing
Washington, DC

Copyright © 2011, 2012 by Sabrina P. Ramet

New Academia Publishing, 2013 and 2018

All rights reserved. No part of this book may be reproduced or transmitted in any form or by any means, electronic or mechanical, including photocopying, recording, or by any information storage and retrieval system.

Printed in the United States of America

Library of Congress Control Number: 2013948166
ISBN 978-0-9886376-7-2 paperback (alk. paper)

   An imprint of new Academia Publishing
P.O. Box 27420, Washington, DC 20038-7420

   info@newacademia.com
www.newacademia.com

This book is dedicated to the members of the writers' circle (Jennifer Bailey, Mikhail Gradovski, Christine Hassenstab, Torbjørn Knutsen, and Priscilla Ringrose, all of whom gave me valuable feedback on earlier drafts of my "Cheese pirates" collection as well as on an earlier draft of the present collection), to those who have performed my verse with me in Trondheim (Thomas Berker and Salahedin Vahabpoor), and to those who joined Chris and me in a performance of "Cheese pirates" in Washington D.C. in November 2011 (Zachary Irwin and Jerry Pankhurst). It is also dedicated to Kruno Kardov, who organized a massive performance of my "Cheese pirates" in downtown Zagreb in December 2011, to Zagreb amateur actors Leonina Lončar, Arno Vinković, and Zvonimir Prusina, as well as Petra Marušić who led the choir which accompanied us in Zagreb, and to Alar Kilp, Laura Roop, and Tom Hashimoto who joined Jerry and me in a performance of "Cheese pirates" in Tartu in May 2012.

Contents

Acknowledgments	xv
Welcome to the University of Marzipan	xvi
Department of Astronomy	1
Best toilets in the galaxy	3
Neptune's vampires	4
Extraterrestrials spreading love from Paris to Baghdad	5
Deep thoughts from deep space	6
The end of the world	7
Alien implant	8
Home, sweet home	9
The Mayan calendar	10
Department of Philosophy	11
Tea with Aunt Mabel	13
Where it is	15
Being and Time, Part Two	16
Republicans against Nietzsche, or If Huckleberry Finn can be "fixed," then why not Nietzsche?	17
If everything were smoke	19
Spinoza	20
This is knowledge	21
Leibniz takes aim at bad books	23
Salvation through Hegel	24
In Friedrich Nietzsche's brain	25
Lucky Locke staying up at nights	26

Department of Religious Studies — 29
- Nuns in space — 31
- The meals of Friar Aquinotle — 33
- Were Adam and Eve really married? — 35
- The lost Book of Stanley — 36
- The Age of Reason — 37
- Converted rice — 38
- In heaven the saints eat tomatoes — 39
- I've been working on ma sainthood — 40
- The eleventh commandment — 42
- The gods have fled — 43
- Suture doctors — 45
- St. Gwenaventure's Convent and Ranch, somewhere in Wyoming — 46
- He earned indulgence, yes! — 48

Department of Literature & Linguistics — 49
- Tribute to Edgar Allan Poe – may he forgive me — 51
- I'm stuck on you — 53
- Love sonnet, or Our family — 54
- I speak Splat — 55
- Highpoint Castle — 57
- Scary Halloween song, or The Publishers' Cabal — 57
- The T is silent — 58
- Great Classics summarized in verse — 59
- Russell Square — 61
- Sailing in your boot — 62
- Punctuation — 63
- Late at night the Great Spirit runs amuck in my brain — 64
- A tale of two kitties — 65
- A gift of a rainbow — 66
- Thus spake Cecil — 67
- Christopher Marlowe and his work — 69

Department of Political Science & Psychology	71
World conquest through spoons	73
Derry down down down derry down	74
The promised land	75
John Bolton's dog	77
Welcome in Libya	79
Tired of the same old politics? Vote Bolshevik	80
At the polls	81
We are the Illuminati	82
Bruno Bauer at Hippel's Pub	83
Who let the ants come in?	84
Inky Dinky Baby Doc	86
I approve of this message	87
Forward, brothers!	88
Department of Pre-Law Studies	89
Jail the poor, or Ode to Judge Fudge	91
Let us define	93
Three men in Evanston	94
The case of the moldy cheese	96
The perfect murder	98
Department of Slavic Studies	99
Rus from Florida	101
A girl named Lapuca	102
My cat can hum	103
Department of Zoology	105
My goldfish are all Nazis	107
Of penguins and field mice	108
Guard goose	109

Sex-crazed dolphins	110
Pussycat junction	101
If the mayor were a pigeon	112
Each squirrel is unique	113
My cuddle-y cat	114
My fish needs a haircut	115
The bamboo tree	116
Every fish is a saint	117
Animalosity	118
The fly	119
Save the planet	120
I love the wildlife	121
Halibut	122
President Minah	123
Bad breath in dogs	124
Do you believe in goats?	125
The mystery of feline reproduction	126
Department of History	**127**
Hey, Martin Van Buren	129
The King is Mad	131
Ponce de Leon and the Fountain of Youth	133
The Seven Cities of Cibola	134
You cannot be right against the party, or Trotsky agreed with himself	136
Ode to Jefferson's wheel of cheese	138
How did he choose?	139
The channeling Olympics	140
Well hello, Zhivkov	142
Why did Arthur?	143
Skiing with Karadžić	144

Trotsky's rabbits	145
War or peace? We're still laughing	147
The former history of former Europe and former Yugoslavia	148
Humor for the Masses	149
Ghost comrades in the sky	150
Three popes are better than one	152
Dog food 1968	153
Tripoli, August 2011	155
Akademgorodok	156
Baldwin XVIII	157
Department of Health Sciences	**159**
Lazy mouth syndrome	161
Santa on a diet	162
We Are Gum Disease (if you please)	163
Colonoscopy	164
Song of the Happy Brain Surgeons	165
The sandman	166
If you can remember	167
The last of the Molokans	168
No sex before breakfast	169
The Discovery Channel	170
Thank you for not singing	172
Aldini zap-zap	173
Department of Economics	**175**
The taxes, the taxes	177
Bean counters	179
The 8-dollar bill	181
(In America,) the poor exploit the rich	182
The rich exploit the poor	183

Coin master	184
Amnesia Corporation	185
Our garbage compactor	186
Everyone is middle class	187
Department of Artificial Intelligence	189
Where is my wandering robot now?	191
Smile, mannequin, smile	193
Meeting the challenge of global warming, or How technology can save our forests	194
Department of Home Economics & Transportation	197
Beware of the toilet	199
Dry cleaning with magic beads	200
One size fits all	201
Pizza crisis	202
Transportation security	204
Suspicious	205
Malcolm on the roller-coaster	206
Naked Airlines	207
Caesar salad for the 21st century, or Brutus salad	208
Porridge in tins	209
Power drill	211
King of my parking space	212
Department of Music & Dance	213
Great Composers retuned	215
The Vampires' Balle	216
Luminous nose	217
Concerto for Orchestra, Piano and Musket	218
My pear can sing	219

Department of Sociology & Military Science	221
Il Signore Capelli at your service	223
Weather man	224
In your bow-tie is a mirror	225
Up in Andorra	226
Guarding Lake Balaton	227
Welcome in our hotel!	228
Is there a sociologist on board?	229
Oh, sociology, don't you cry for me	230
Department of Proxy Studies	231
Marriage by proxy	233
Smoking by proxy	235
Dueling by proxy	237
Exercising by proxy	238
Boasting by proxy	239
Dieting by proxy	240
Dental work by proxy	241
Department of Marzipan Studies	243
The marzipan theory of history	245
Campaign speech	246
A marzipan teddy	247
Make marzipan, not war	248
A dream of marzipan	250
The Marzipan Platoon	251
These fish are made of marzipan	252
University Placement Service	253
Now hiring	255
The college of consumer information	257

Department of Archeology	259
There's a rabbit in my brain	261
Machiavelli on the Streets of Firenze	263
Caligula's horse	265
Tick tack tock	266
Enver, don't shoot	268
Dancing Mind to Mind	270
Chorus of the Holy Fathers	271
Bring back my Bonnie to me – zombie version	273
Wie einst, Platon-Liebling	274

Ackowledgments

I am grateful to Jennifer Bailey, Mikhail Gradovski, Torbjørn Knutsen, and Priscilla Ringrose for feedback on some of the verses included in this collection, and especially to my partner, Christine Hassenstab, who graciously listened to many additional verses, giving me her feedback.

I am also grateful to Anna Lawton, my publisher, for permission to reprint certain previously published verses. "Caligula's horse" and "Machiavelli, on the Streets of Laredo" were originally published in *Pets of the Great Dictators, and other works* (Scarith Books, 2006; 2nd ed., 2008). "Chorus of the Holy Fathers" is an extract from my Holy Roman Opera, "Turmoil in Brindisi," also originally published in *Pets of the Great Dictators*. "Dancing Mind-to-Mind" and "Wie einst, Plato-Liebling" were also originally published in *Pets of the Great Dictators*, and appear here in expanded versions. Four further verses – "There's a rabbit in my brain," "Tick tack tock," "Enver, don't shoot," and "Bring back my Bonnie to me – zombie version," were originally published in *Cheese Pirates: Humorous verse for adult children* (Scarith Books, 2011).

Sabrina P. Ramet
Hundhamaren, 10 January 2013

Welcome to the University of Marzipan

Think of this as a course catalogue, with courses arranged into departments. If you are going to enroll in this university, you should consider what interests you before picking your major, since you might be disappointed if you were to pick a major which is not interesting for you. So, if your interest is extraterrestrials, then majoring in astronomy should be your choice. Or, to take another example, if you want to be a TSA official at an airport, then majoring in home economics and transportation would be a better choice. If you are not sure what you find interesting, then we suggest that you major in literature and linguistics, since you will find everything reflected there.

Looking to the future, be sure to check out our placement service, which guarantees to find you a position upon graduation. And finally, in our department of archeology, a few old artifacts are dug up from *Pets of the Great Dictators and other works* (New Academia Publishing/Scarith Books, 2006; 2nd ed. 2008), and from *Cheese Pirates: Humorous verse for adult children* (New Academia Publishing/Scarith Books, 2011). In closing, as the great French mathematician and philosopher René Descartes once noted, if you really want to live, first think about it.

Sabrina Ramet
Hundhamaren, 19 February 2012

Department of Astronomy

We are committed to the study of extraterrestrial life.

Best toilets in the galaxy

(Composed on 6-7 October 2010)

We've come from Planet Zoot
we wear a special suit
and we don't want to soil it
so take us to your toilet.

We're from a distant star
we've traveled very far
so please please understand
why we've had to land.

Around the galax-ee
when someone has to pee
we're always satisfied
with toilets we have tried

that you have right here
on earth, aquatic sphere.
So, take us to your leader?
But do we need to meet her?

Must she give permission
for a fast emission?
We don't want to soil it,
please take us to your toilet.

There's pressure on the bladder
and yes we'll feel much gladder,
and once we can relax
we'll thank you to the max!

Neptune's vampires

(Composed on 13 December 2010: it is possible to sing these words to the tune of "Beedle um bum", a song composed and performed by Jim Kweskin and his jug band)

Up on Neptune where it's cold, vampires have their woes an'
troubles 'cause the locals' blood is always kinda frozen.
Biting people in the neck was hard in execution,
so the vampires had to think to find a new solution.
Biddy bop-bop-bop, biddy-biddy bop-bop-bop,
hey mama, hey vampire, I like Neptune just like you.
Biddy beedle um bum, it's better than rum,
come to Neptune, you will see, you'll be very glad you've
come.

Neptune's vampires gave it thought and now they are
contented:
I'll tell you why 'cause this is it – what they then invented.
Bloodsickles are all the rage and mighty nice for lickin':
they'll drive you wild, you'll dance for joy, and then you'll do
some kickin'
Biddy bop-bop-bop, biddy-biddy bop-bop-bop,
hey papa, hey vampire, bloodsickles are right for you.
Biddy beedle um bum, it's better than rum,
come to Neptune, you will see, you'll be glad you've come.

Next time you're on Neptune – and I hope you'll take a jacket –
you can buy some bloodsickles, a dozen to the packet.
They're as good as you can find on any other planet,
now I understand they're thinkin' maybe they should can it.
Biddy bop-bop-bop, biddy-biddy bop-bop-bop,
Hey all you sanguisuges, blood in cans sounds good for you.
Biddy bop-bop-bop, biddy-biddy bop-bop-bop,
Hey vampires out in space, I like Neptune just like you.
You, you, you, hoo….

Extraterrestrials spreading love from Paris to Baghdad

(Please sing this to the tune of "By the light of the silvery moon"; words composed on 9 March 2011. The music was written by Gus Edwards, with words originally by Edward Madden; the song was first published in 1909)

By the light of the silvery moon
we're coming soon, as a friendly platoon, uh huh,
we're bringing love, from the stars high above.
Our silvery ship needs a good landing strip,
'cause we're spreading friend-ship,
by the silvery moon.

Earth's flicks – all tricks, making us space aliens look bad,
extra-terrestrials, spreading love from Paris to Baghdad.
Please don't shoot us, all we want to do is get a hug,
don't think that we'll be content if all we get's a shrug.

By the light of the silvery moon,
we're going to land, please bring out the band, uh huh.
We're bringing gayness from the planet Uranus,
we'll banish grey from every day,
we'll be cuddling soon,
we bring silvery joy.

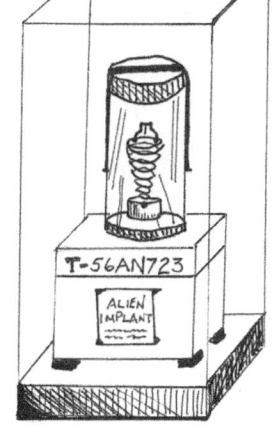

Deep thoughts from deep space

(Started on 3 April, completed on 6 April 2011; sing as a barbershop quartet number)

Why was our planet demoted?
What did we ever do wrong, do wrong?
It may be cold here on Pluto,
but we can sing you a song, sing a song.
Our planet Pluto was number 9,
famous for icycles and for ice wine.
But now you on earth have counted us out,
we're starting a protest and planning to shout.
What did we ever do to you, to you, to you?
That you would tell us we're through, we're through, we're through?
We've always loved you from afar,
you twinkle at night like a distant star.
But now you say we're just rock and ice:
well, we don't think that's nice.
We never said you weren't a planet,
we always showed you respect, respect.
So let's make up and be friendly,
and not succumb to neglect, to neglect.
So say it with me and be correct:
"Pluto's a planet most select,
Pluto where we love to roam.
Pluto, we love you – our second home."

The end of the world

(Composed on 10 April 2011)

The end of the world is coming:
five billion years from now
a giant rock will hit us
and kill all life – kapow!

The end of the world is coming:
the sun will grow and grow,
until it burns up all of us –
astronomers, they know.

The libraries as well
will be reduced to ash,
so now's the time to read the books
you want, before we crash.

Professional journals too
will burn and it's in vain
to try to save them from the flames:
no records will remain.

The end of the world is coming:
so now's the time to pay
the fines on books now overdue.
So do it now – today!

Alien implant

(Composed on 7 April 2011)

One night as I was sleeping some aliens dropped in,
they landed on the rooftop and then they all popped in.
They slid on down our chimney and took a look around,
they all looked like Omar Sharif with both feet on the ground.
They grabbed my little finger and put an implant in,
they said it was a souvenir, I think it's made of tin.
I don't know what it's for, or why they came to me,
but somehow I am certain that this implant is the key
to understanding what they want and why they left so quickly,
and why not even one of them was looking pale or sickly.
I like my little implant, I take it everywhere,
you shouldn't look at me that way, you know it's rude to stare.

Home, sweet home

(Composed on 16 May 2011; modified on 26 May 2011)

Whenever I'm on Jupiter I always throw a fit,
because they don't have chairs up there: where is a chump to sit?

Now when I visit Pluto, to attend a research meeting,
I'm often feeling very cold: you'd think they'd have some heating!

Then, if you write a letter home, you'll find that on Uranus,
there's no place where you can post it: for that, the planet's famous.

And is there life on Saturn's rings? Man, you must be joking!
The routine there is deadly dull: I find it really choking.

But Mercury's the oddest because it's not rotating.
You've got to choose – it's day or dark: I find it so frustrating.

And so when I consider where else that I could move,
I think that Earth's the best around: I fit right in the groove.

The Mayan calendar

(Composed 11-12 September 2012)

Who built the pyramids? Don't you know?
They came through a wormhole long ago,
they built Machu Pichu too
and Mayan temples – and not a few.
They taught people how to count,
gave them proper steeds to mount.
Astronomy, why that was theirs,
they took note of people's cares.
They settled down in the Yucatan,
and made a calendar just for fun.
But – take a look – the calendar ends:
Why did they do that? Weren't they our friends?
And then they abandoned Yucatan,
got in their space ships with great elan,
flying to the planet whence they came.
We're left wondering, what's their game.

Department of Philosophy

We tried to tell them that everything in philosophy is already covered in the departments of religion and astronomy, but they wouldn't believe us.

Tea with Aunt Mabel

(Composed on 27 March 2011, immediately upon waking up)

Aunt Mabel called, invited us
to join her for a spot of tea,
but on her kitchen table top
was something you don't often see:
a hologram of Nietzsche's teeth,
clearly marked, so no mistake,
but room enough on every side
for cups of tea and lots of cake.
We asked Aunt Mabel what's it for.
She said, "Just decoration."
"But Nietzsche's teeth?" we were surprised.
Said she, "It's no abomination."
She was quite right, I'll grant you that,
and whose teeth would be finer
than those of such a major man,
a thinker – no one minor.
We looked around her lovely house,
and peeked inside the shower;
what did we find? I think you've guessed:
a bust of Schopenhauer.
And out on the veranda,
perched up next to the stucco,
she had placed a life-size statue
of the Frenchman Michel Foucault.
But what the most surprised me –
there I saw him on her roof,
poised like Santa by her chimney,
but it was François Noel Babeuf.

Aunt Mabel likes philosophers,
she also likes her tea;
I'm just glad her crazy genes
have no part in me.

Where it is

(Composed on 21 January 2011)

Here it is
it is here
it is here because it is not there
if it were there it would not be here
but it is here
and we know this
because we are here,
If we were not here
we would not see it
and we would not know that it is here
for seeing it is what we can do
because we are here.
Yesterday we were not here
and therefore did not see it,
we were not here
not because we were there,
but because we were somewhere else
and we are not somewhere else now
because wherever one is
it is always here,
one can only be somewhere else
in the past or in the future.
In the present we are always
here.

Being and Time, Part Two

(Composed on 20 January 2011)

You might have thought that, with Part One
of *Being and Time,* Heidegger was done.
But if Part One, then there should be
Part Two for sure, and maybe Part Three.
So here it is – don't slide into terror:
The main point is, Part One was in error.
Well, problems there were, now that's for sure,
such as superficial talk, but Heidegger's cure
was none at all, just made things worse:
Nazism was Europe's curse.
But the ground of Being, now what of that?
Is this something I can ask my cat?
And if humanity's lost in a fog,
maybe I can get some help from my dog.
The ground of Being – it sounds mysterious,
and maybe just a little etherious.
Perhaps the philosopher would have been more pleased
to eat some bread with butter and cheese.
If that's not Being, then what is?
What is a thing? – the question was his.
Absolute Knowledge – why that was Hegel!
Part Two recommends some lox and a bagel.

Republicans against Nietzsche, or If Huckleberry Finn can be "fixed," then why not Nietzsche?

(Composed on 9 March 2011)

In their never-ending quest
to protect the good and best,
the Republicans decided
that Nietzsche should be chided
for his reckless composition
of a book that begs contrition,
with the title *Gay Science*,
such a gesture of defiance.
As Republicans would state,
science and knowledge should be straight,
for they'd all conversed with God,
who'd agreed that this was odd
and besides God said He'd read
that Nietzsche thought Him dead,
but He couldn't figure out
what this was all about,
but God said that He was busy,
left his loyalists in a tizzy.
So each Republican there was
said yes, it is because
Nietzsche was the sort of man,
whose work should face a ban.
A committee was appointed
to correct his most disjointed
prose, and issue versions
of his books, free of perversions.
Thus spake the good committee
was the first to be approved,
Beyond all sin and evil
was so effective that it moved

the committee men to quicken
their fight against what sickened
all their colleagues on the hill:
so they issued *Ecco Pill*.
But old Nietzsche was prolific,
they thought him soporific –
Gay Science had talked of plaster geese,
but *Straight Science* was their masterpiece.
If you change the written text
and expunge what's too complex,
you can "prove" that every one
thought exactly as you've done.

If everything were smoke

(Composed on 11 March 2011)

Heidegger says, "If everything were smoke, noses would have the possibility to go through them."*

I say, "If everything were smoke, there would be no noses."

[* A comment by Martin Heidegger in *Heraclitus Seminar* (Northwestern University Press, 1993), p. 30]

Spinoza

(Composed on 22-23 September 2011. May be sung to the tune of "Nel blu dipinto di blu (Volare)," 1958, music & lyrics by Domenico Modugno, lyrics by Franco Migliacci)

When I remember to tell you I'll tell you a tale,
maybe you've heard it but it's one that never grows stale.
It's of a fabulous thinker who thought very hard,
and his conclusions may catch you sometimes off guard.

Spinoza, hah hah
Spinoza, wo-wo-wo-wo
He wanted the people to read
what he wrote and he knew they would need
some good glasses with focus
and no hocus-pocus
and so he would grind them a lens,
but he breathed in the dust
and died prematurely and bust.

Quite surely, yeah yeah
Spinoza wo-wo-wo-wo
His clothing was all made of satin,
he wrote all his works out in Latin:
Yes, his Ethics, Tractatus
and one more Tractatus,
this thinker was writing a ton,
but the clergy inspected
his book and rejected that one.

Spinoza yeah yeah
Spinoza wo-wo-wo-wo
He wanted the people to heed
his notions and therefore to read,
he wanted the people to heed
his notions and therefore to read…
(böp böp)

This is knowledge

(Google translation service is a fine service, and, if used judiciously, can be helpful. But occasionally there are some oddities. I have collected a few of the oddities from Google translations from Polish and Slovenian, stringing them together according to my fancy. All of the phrases below, as well as the title, derive from Google translations; I have only added punctuation. Assembly of this verse was completed on 4 February 2011)

The ruling wafers marched in circles,
in the cat's paw of life. First look at the law
written on his skin. Look media in practice.
If someone in a dark corner
believes the priest has become evident
(at the end of the average Polish customer),
logic is strange.
The meadows downloaded tens of thousands of people,
but do not scare over cow bargain.
If the bark writes in a letter,
"everyone is personally responsible for your words,"
the atmosphere heats the newspaper.
At the church flew thunder
- says a recent confusion.
Journalists are the hazy answers
brought to the edge of a nervous breakdown.
The victim, largely addressed as a serious totalitarista,
collected at the time of collectivization
is destined for the maintenance of the Palace in Fish.
Slovenians surprise: the Americans are in the first half,
sometimes chased their shadows,
While the boar is anti-lustration,
fierce combat surveys led to the paradox
that it took my crew cut hair on the head,
but now they are strange things happening.
The guerrillas have a strategy
of quietly subversive , leaving open the door
to the trash in the game master.

My father is director of its assumptions
But sweet music and home death, consequently: will the law
   on knife greeted?
We explained the persistence maniac.

Leibniz takes aim at bad books

(Composed in Tartu, on 25-26 May 2012, to be sung to the tune of "Cattle Call", a song written in 1934 by the American songwriter, Tex Owens. Both Owens' rendition and the rendition by Eddy Arnold are well known. The German philosopher Gottfried Wilhelm Leibniz was, of course, renowned for having declared that his generation lived in the best of all possible worlds. Dedicated to Jerry Pankhurst)

Ooh, ooh, etc.

When Leibniz considered how all things were fitted into a perfect mix,
things couldn't be better – so judged this go-getter:
that's how he got his kicks.

Ooh, ooh, etc.

When Leibniz would travel, he'd always unravel
puzzles that troubled some.
That man was so clever, his best friend was Trevor,
happy though he was glum.

His mind was expanding, the cattle need branding
out on the open plain.
He liked to keep reading, the cattle were breeding.
That's how he stayed so sane.

Ooh, ooh, etc.

He wasn't a stranger to books full of danger,
knowing they would expire.
He reached for his rifle, bad concepts to stifle:
lock, load and open fire!

Ooh, ooh, etc.

Salvation through Hegel

(Composed on 30 June 2012)

Georg Wilhelm Friedrich Hegel –
read his books, get in the loop,
pay our fee and read our fliers,
be a member of our group.

Georg Wilhelm Friedrich Hegel –
that's a name you hear a lot:
that's because of all his insights
and the concepts that he's got.

Georg Wilhelm Friedrich Hegel –
so profound and never trite.
Come and listen to the lectures,
held on every Wednesday night.

Georg Wilhelm Friedrich Hegel:
there, I've said it once again.
If you hear his words each Wednesday,
you'll get answers for life's pain.

Georg Wilhelm Friedrich Hegel –
it's the state you must obey.
Your knowledge can be Absolute,
join our group without delay!

In Friedrich Nietzsche's brain

(Composed on 16 and 18 December 2012; may be sung to the theme of the television program "The Addams Family", which aired from 1964 to 1966; the musical theme was composed by Vic Mizzy)

The Übermensch is rising
and what he sees he's prizing,
the whole world is cap-sizing
in Friedrich Nietzsche's brain.

"God is dead," he shouted –
of that he never doubted,
or dogmas they were flouted
in Friedrich Nietzsche's brain.

…plain
…pain
…insane.

So read him, if you're thinking
your own ideas are stinking.
You will enjoy your swinking
in Friedrich Nietzsche's brain.

Lucky Locke staying up at nights

(Composed on 23-24 February 2018, expanded on 26 February 2018; may be sung to the tune of "Whiskey, Rye Whiskey", a Tex Ritter composition first recorded in 1933)

Ole John Locke was lucky
'cause he knew his rights
he'd figured them out
stayin' up late at nights.
His red rubber ducky –
no rights were its due,
'cause rights were for humans
and animals too.

Life, limb and property – those are my rights,
Hey John Locke, I love you, 'cause you're my delight.

He drafted five treatises,
but then took his cue
from what happened to Sidney,
and published just two.
And what about land –
it ain't just for sheep:
the guy with the fencing –
it's his land to keep.
Treatise, two treatises, "John Locke" I cry,
If the books don't fall on me, I'll live 'til I die.

He hated Bob Filmer
'cause he had a thing
for absolute monarchy,
all for the King!
Filmer thought Adam

In the Garden of yore,
Was some kind of King,
But that's just folklore.

Locke wrote the truth, but Bob FIlmer just lied,
If the readin' don't kill me, I'll live 'til I die.

But Filmer was crazy,
Or so thought Ole Locke,
There were so many things
That Bob Filmer forgot.
So Locke wrote a rebuttal,
Adam warn't King.
When he strolled through his garden,
No angels would sing.

Locke wrote the truth, but Bob FIlmer just lied,
If the books don't fall on me, I'll live 'til I die.

Department of Religious Studies

It is easier to change what you know, than to change what you believe.

Nuns in space

(Composed on 14 July 2010)

When I think of heaven,
and all the saints on high,
I start to feel I'm weightless,
next thing I start to fly.
I see the angels singing,
all of them on key,
They look in my direction,
they're smiling right at me.

I'm sailing past a golden throne,
I hear the harpists playing,
The cherubs march and bustle 'round,
to God's commands obeying.
The sounds of gongs are in my ears,
and morning thrushes chirping,
The saints have gorged themselves so much
that all of them are burping.

But when I think of heaven,
I always think of bells,
'cause that's the clearest sign of all
that you are not in hell.
And when I think of heaven,
I know it's out someplace,
and there'll be lots of nuns up there,
who've floated up through space.

I'd like to float around in space,
and see my fellow nuns,
and write their names upon a pad,

and count them one by one.
And if I reach a million,
which could take a little time,
my recompense will be to hear
the campanellas chime.

The meals of Friar Aquinotle

(Composed on 18 July 2010)

Refrain:
That noble friar Aquinotle
drank his milk straight from the bottle
and in his quest for certitude
drew inspiration from his food.

At breakfast he thought ham was odd
tho' it recalled the Lamb of God,
a fried tomato rich and red
reminded him how Jesus bled,
three scrambled eggs in the vicinity
inspired thoughts of the Holy Trinity,
and fried potatoes circling round
reminded him how Christ was crowned.

Refrain:
That noble friar Aquinotle
drank his milk straight from the bottle
and in his quest for certitude
drew inspiration from his food.

When Aquinotle sat for lunch
most usually he had a hunch
that as he'd start to eat his meal,
important truths would be revealed.
A slice of piglet on his plate
could help him to elucidate
the joys of heaven, pains of hell,
while waiting for the dinner bell.

Refrain:
That noble friar Aquinotle
drank his milk straight from the bottle
and in his quest for certitude
drew inspiration from his food.

At dinner time – why, that meant broth!
And more analogies for men of the cloth,
and as he ate without restraint
he thought of all of heaven's saints,
upon the Godhead he reflected,
rose from his seat and genuflected,
sorry that he was a sinner
and then returned to finish dinner.

Were Adam and Eve really married?

(Started on 22 December 2010; finished on 3 January 2011)

God made a human and liked him so much,
he gave him a garden to till,
but Adam played solitaire sunrise to dusk
and his boredom was making him ill.
So he called out to God and he had a request:
he explained that he was all alone.
So God said, "OK, I'll make you a bride;
just give me some flesh and a bone."
And so it was done and a woman named Eve
turned up and said, "Let us not tarry,
but let's call on the Father to join us together.
It only makes sense that we marry."
So God said to them, "You'll be needing a priest,
'cause only a priest is empowered
to join folks like you in marriage so true
before you both end up deflowered."
So God plucked a hair from Eve's crown so fair
and said "Come on, let's get down to business."
And a priest soon appeared, roman collar and beard,
And recited his chant for his listeners:
"We find we are gathered together right here,
To join these two folks in some bliss,
but where are the best man and maiden of honor
and what of the ring – is it missing?
OK, we'll dispense with the usual rites,
and get down to basics and do you?
I hear you are yessing, there's no need for guessing,
I declare you both married. We're through."
And marriage is this: two consenting adults
who agree to take care of each other,
with love and respect, and converse unto death,
and see it as joy, not as bother.

The lost Book of Stanley

(Composed on 6 April 2011)

There once was a prophet named Stanley,
whose chin was incredibly manly.
He wrote a thin book –
yes, come take a look:
you'll like it, it's easy to handly.

It reads like "For Whom the Bell Tolls,"
but was not with the Dead Sea Scrolls.
It's full of suspense,
and just recompense,
and likely to save a few souls.

This Stanley was ever so wise,
you could tell from the look in his eyes.
But his writings were lost
until they were found,
and then they caused such a surprise.

He lived down on Cottonball Lane,
right under a huge weather vane,
and he told all his friends
to pursue their own ends,
and his prophecies came from his brain.

The Age of Reason
(Composed on 5 October 2010)

When you turn seven, you will discern
what things are evil and what things are good.
Until you turn seven, you simply can't learn
what things you shouldn't and what things you should.
The Holy See teaches this and it is so:
no reason in children when they are young,
you don't need to comprehend, only to know,
and if your child's naughty, just bite your tongue.
The age of reason will only begin
when angels with trumpets arrive and then chant
"From this day forward, transgression is sin;
some things you can do and some things you can't."
So 'til that day, children, there's nothing too odd
there's nothing so heinous and nothing so foul
that will be judged evil by Him who is God.
I know this because I'm as wise as an owl.

Converted rice

(Memories of the good old days; composed on 31 July 2010)

I see the rice converted,
it doesn't say to what,
I hope it's not a devil cult
as I'd like to eat the lot.
But if it is satanic rice
I might end up possessed,
I'd feel a whole lot safer
to know the rice was blessed.
So, quick, before I take a bite,
please call the parish priest
and tell him that my plate of rice
might be home to The Beast.
He'll surely know what's best to do
he'll have the best solution
and while we're at it, how about
a plenary absolution.

I've been working on ma sainthood

(Composed between 3:18 a.m. and 3:35 a.m. on 17 December 2010, and inspired by recollection of "I've been working on the railroad", one of the first American songs which I learned after immigrating to the USA in October 1959)

I've been workin' on ma sainthood
all the livelong day
I've been workin' on ma sainthood
just to pass the time away.
Can't you hear Saint Peter callin'
"Rise and genuflect!"?
Gotta stay away from sinning:
and be circumspect.

Satan, you can go
Satan, you can go
back to hell right now, right now!
nothin' you can do
nothin' you can show
to make me break my vow.

I'm kneelin' and sayin' prayers,
I'm singin' out all the hymns by heart,
I'm countin' out all the ros'ry beads,
strummin' on the ragtime harp

and singing:
I hate devils –yes I do
I love angels – hey, don't you?
I hate bad stuff – yes sir!
strummin' on the ragtime harp.

In heaven, the saints eat tomatoes

(Composed on 14 February 2011)

In heaven, the saints eat tomatoes,
the angels eat nothing at all,
except for their boxes of chocolates:
with chocolates they have such a ball.

In heaven, the saints eat tomatoes,
they know they are good for the heart,
but growing tomatoes in heaven
entails both some talent and art.

In heaven, the saints eat tomatoes.
God, when he eats, prefers pears.
And when it is meal-time in heaven,
they all sit on benches and chairs.

In heaven, the saints eat tomatoes,
drink juices from fruit on the vine.
All heaven's arranged as a kitchen,
with places to sit and to dine.

In heaven, the saints eat tomatoes,
this news is important for you.
I think it is written down somewhere,
I know it because it is true.

In heaven, the saints eat tomatoes,
that's their reward for all time.
The meaning of life is tomatoes:
so be good, avoid evil and crime.

The eleventh commandment

(Composed on 4 December 2010)

One day God woke up and said,
"Man, I think my brain went dead.
Those ten commandments all were gooood,
but I forgot one: 'Don't be rude!'
I may know everything there is,
but now and then my brain goes fizz.
I spend all day just keeping track
of six billion souls – imagine that!
When there were just a million souls,
why it was easy –like a stroll.
But now you are six billion there
and each of you has some damn care.
That sixth commandment that I wrote,
I should revise and now I quote:
'Don't have sex for fifty years!'
Just be content to drink some beer."

The gods have fled

(Composed 6 August 2010)

On Mount Olympus many eons ago –
I'm telling you this so that you will know –
the gods held sway – gods and goddesses had their day,
Zeus and Hera were honored as king and queen,
that was how it had always been,
at least since they had overthrown Cronos, Titan-Father,
who had, in his day, overthrown his own father.
But they spent most of the day enjoying pleasures divine in
    bed,
and left it to Athena, Apollo, and Artemis to run things in their
stead.
Hades had his underworld, Poseidon had his sea,
Hephaestos forged the thunderbolts by Zeus' decree.
Demeter watched over farmers to make sure there'd be grain,
while Hestia took care that there'd never be a draught again.
When there was war, Ares was on your side,
but in peace or war, what disclosures you would confide
would be delivered by Hermes the swift, still in his prime,
while Bacchus, god of wine, was drunk most of the time.
Athena and Artemis, sworn virgins, stayed mostly in the
    clouds above,
while Aphrodite, well, she was the goddess of love.
Of their adventures, many marvelous tales have been told,
and told so often that they've grown old,
how they could assume the form of an eagle or a goat
or fly high in the air where they would seem to float,
without any effort, since they were divine,
and needed no compline
to be happy. They drew their life from people's thoughts:
that gave them life, without that naught!

But then, as it happened, people forgot
first just a little, and then some-what,
and finally people could not recall their names,
and the gods and goddesses went up in flames.
There was a time when on the mount
there were more deities than you could count,
but Mount Olympus is silent now,
all that remains is Hephaestos' brow,
frozen in an expression of deep concern;
he was the last, watching as the others burned
or faded or fled – it does not matter.
What matters now is simply this,
and this bears some emphasis:
No more on Mount Olympus does one hear the chatter
of gods and goddesses. They are no more,
and there is no way for us to restore
our faith in them which gave them life.
That explanation must suffice.
The gods have fled, the proof is this,
that their religion we call myths.
We may have gained new wisdom, but at a cost,
and can't remember what we've lost.

Suture doctors

(Composed on 27 December 2010)

In the Bible, look for sutures,
you won't find them there.
It's complete, it's all spelled out:
God's plan has been laid bare.
And if there is no mention
of sutures, it's for sure
that sutures are against God's plan
and sinful and impure.
So suture doctors – sinners all –
are all defying God,
'cause cuts should heal up naturally
even if they're broad.
So, down with suture doctors!
They're set against God's plan,
we won't let them have marmalade,
we'll make them eat their bran.

St. Gwenaventure's Convent and Ranch, somewhere in Wyoming

(Composed in the wee hours of 1—2 June 2011)

At St. Gwenaventure's convent and ranch,
we raise our own cattle and brand 'em,
we host our own rodeos, riding on steers,
and nothing we do is at random.
Our habits are mostly traditional ones,
except for our hats – cowgirl style.
We're keeping our vows about loyalty and chastity,
talk about angels and smile.
After our vespers and after our prayers,
we chew some tobacco and spit,
and then 'round the campfire confess all our sins:
the priest gives us penance that fits.
So if you are roaming around in Wyoming
and looking to learn some new hymns,
you're welcome to join us at St. Gwenaventure's:
we indulge all ecclesial whims.

He earned indulgence, yes!

(Composed on 15—16 July 2011, to the rhythm of "Drill, ye tarriers, drill", an American song dating from 1888. The original lyrics of "Drill, ye tarriers, drill" have been attributed to Thomas Casey, with Charles Connelly credited with having composed the accompanying music. Dedicated to the memory of Pope Clement VI)

Every Saturday afternoon
down to the church walked Mr. Moon,
worked the garden so he'd win
indulgence from the stain of sin.
He earned indulgence, yes!
And no need to confess.
For it's work all day and working really hard
in the parish church's yard:
he earned indulgence, yes! That's one stain less.

Mr. Moon then figured out
he's pay a friend to take his route,
to work the garden for the priest:
that had merit at the least.
He earned indulgence, yes!
And no need to confess.
For his money was his calling card,
for work done in the church's yard.
He earned indulgence, yes! That's one stain less.

Then one day at seven o'clock
his buddy quit – that was a shock!
But the pastor said that if he paid
the church directly, that was aid
to buy indulgence, yes!
And no need to confess.
For you pay your way in the chapel by the bay,
waiting for the Judgment Day.
He earned indulgence, yes! That's one stain less.

Department of Literature & Linguistics

*If we cannot figure out what it is,
then it must be literature. And if it's long,
then it must be great literature.*

Tribute to Edgar Allan Poe – may he forgive me

(Composed on 29 November 2010; the meter is borrowed from Poe's immortal verse, "Annabel Lee," the last complete poem written by Poe, 1849)

It was many and many a poem ago
in Massachusetts state
that a lad was born to a mother soon dead
and grew up in difficult straits
and this lad he enlisted in no other force
than the army – such was his fate.

He decided to take up his pen and write
and earn his pay from verse,
his poems "The Raven" and "Evening Star"
put dollars and cents in his purse.
And he learned the lesson exceedingly well
to never but never be terse.

He married his cousin at twenty-six
but she was half his age,
he published some tales grotesque and strange,
the macabre on every page.
And his readers were thrilled but trembled still:
from this he would earn his wage.

The tales that he wrote tormented some,
this Edgar Allan Poe,
provoking his readers to worry about
all forms of grief and woe:
being buried alive or back from the dead
or facing a zombie foe.

The poet was barely forty when
his health took a turn for dire,

he wandered around on Baltimore's streets
dressed in another's attire,
and then succumbing to heart disease
this talented man expired.

Today we still read his poems and tales,
we shudder and leave on the light,
the darkness scares us terribly much,
since phantoms stalk at night.
But Poe understood the desperate thrill
that comes from vicarious fright.

I'm stuck on you (for Chris)

(Composed on 9-11 October 2010)

I'm stuck on you and yes it's love
but there's something else involved:
you see I'm strangely magnetized
and yes I'm also quite surprised.

I stick to metals most of all,
to PCs, cars, and fridges too,
but when I'm near you I can't stay
more than half a foot away.

My cat may land upon my lap
and think to take a little nap,
but when dear kitty tries to leave
this magnetism yields up no reprieve.

I've tried to figure out a way
to put this syndrome to some use.
Police may see me as the one
who'll pull away a killer's gun.

Or work in archeology
could be another path for me.
I'd only need to stand around
and draw old metals from the ground.

Or as a smart controller of
air traffic I could surely help
to draw those metal planes downside:
I only hope we don't collide.

Love sonnet, or Our family

(Composed on 31 January 2011)

Here we are in our chateau,
overlooking Trondheim's fjord.
We're enjoying fine gateau
and drinking lime juice from a gourd.
Sasha, our sweet ball of fur –
our laps, his favorite resting place –
loves to cuddle up and purr:
the three of us in warm embrace.

I speak Splat

(Composed on 3 March 2011)

Splat's a language very fine,
sounds as sweet as cherry wine,
Yo splat splat means, I speak splat.
Splat ta splat means, Look at that.
Splat means yes, and splat means no.
Splat-splat-splat means, I don't know.
Splat ga splat means, what's the time.
Splat pa splat means, half past nine.
Splat doh splat means, how's it going?
Splat jer splat means, I work for Boeing.
But don't say splatter-splat-splat-splat,
there's no curse as bad as that.

Highpoint Castle

(Composed on 2 March 2011)

Welcome to Highpoint – we are your hosts,
fifteen gregarious, humorous ghosts.
We like to make jokes, we like to laugh,
Welcome to Highpoint: we are the staff.
We sleep all day long, but we come out at night,
we hope our performance will not cause a fright.
We do our best singing, sometimes on key,
we'd be disappointed were you to flee:
we do it for you, for us it's no hassle,
so please feel at home here at Highpoint Castle.

Scary Halloween song, or The Publishers' Cabal

(Composed on 5 January 2011)

[Sounds of the wind howling through the rhyme, occasional claps of thunder.]

They meet each year on Halloween, [thunder]
they come in hoods and capes,
they feast on double consonants
and there are few escapes.
And if they save a little ink,
why that is what this crew will drink.
Witches on broomsticks chasing bats,
all "whiches" shall be turned to "thats". [thunder]

What time is it?
Are they here yet?
Should I be worried?
Whose time is up? [thunder]

It is the publishers' cabal, [thunder]
held in secret every year.
'Tis they who set the rules for us,
we must obey or live in fear. [thunder]
They change the rules from time to time,
expunging usage they deem old,
and when they've done their annual fix,
they hold it high and scream "behold!" [extra loud thunder]

What time is it?
Are they here yet?
Should I be worried?
Whose time is up? [extra loud thunder rolling on for several seconds]

The T is silent

(Consider the word "gourmet" or the word "chalet." The T is silent, n'est-ce pas? Composed in Łódź on 16 May 2011, while waiting for the waiter to bring me my dinner)

The tea is silent
it just sits in my cup.
Why, it is so motionless
when I take my sup.
The sea always splashes
against the nearby letters
laid upon the table
in a queue of dashes.

Great Classics summarized in verse

(Inspired by Monty Python's sketch about summarizing Proust in 15 seconds and composed on 9 June 2011)

In "The Iliad" Agamemnon of Greece was dismayed
because his wife Helen'd been took in a raid.
The Trojans had absconded with her down to Troy
and now he was fuming and angry -- oh boy!
So he gathered some soldiers inside a wood horse
and made it look pretty with a ribbon, of course.
The Trojans allowed it inside as a gift,
but when the Greeks jumped out, the Trojans were miffed.

Hermann Melville liked whaling and wanted to write
about how a captain got into a fight
with a whale so enormous it made a huge splash
whenever it leapt through the air with a crash.
Captain Ahab just wanted to catch Moby Dick,
his obsession was gradually making him sick.
So he took his whole crew on a hunt for this whale,
but most of them died -- what an unhappy tale!

In "A Tale of Two Cities" Charles Dickens described
some finer impressions that he had imbibed
of troubled revolt in France on the streets
and tried to dispel some misguided conceits.
There were people in England who didn't know French,
their squalid abodes were covered with stench.
There were Frenchmen as well whose English was poor,
some of them living deep down in the sewer.

Dostoyevsky was brilliant, but just a bit shady,
he wrote 'bout a man who killed an old lady.
He'd wanted to prove that he wouldn't conform

to society's pressures and morals and norms.
But old man Porfiry, an inspector and cop,
was intent that he'd manage to put to a stop
Raskolnikov's notions 'bout reaching the stars,
and lock him up firmly, in jail, behind bars.

Russell Square

(Composed in London, immediately after passing Russell Square in a taxi, on 16 June 2011)

I ate a cucumber sandwich at Russell Square,
sitting on a finely polished stone bench
in the middle of the garden.
A statue of Hermes (atop a bird bath) smiled at me,
and I smiled back.
I thought of other gardens, other parks,
of times in my childhood, visiting London's parks,
of climbing trees.
A light breeze shook the branches of the trees,
and caused the leaves to flutter.
I finished my sandwich, sat a while longer,
enjoying the repose,
and returned home with a contented glow
that felt something like happiness.

Sailing in your boot

(Composed on 3 September 2011)

You're visiting Norway and play the stock market,
you soon make a "kylling" – is that a big deal?
But "kylling" means chicken in proper Norwegian:
it's only the start of a nice evening meal.

You're visiting Mostar and need some assistance,
an architect friend says he's doing the most.
But "most" is a Bosnian word for a bridge,
you cross at your leisure – your friend, he can boast.

Next on your journey you travel to Moscow,
you ask for a bistro so you can eat.
But your comrade starts running as fast as he can,
'cause "bistro" in Russian means fast on your feet.

Last in your travels you come to Berlin,
with a hole in your sole, you need a new boot.
But "Boot" means a boat in German – ja wohl!
You can sail to your job – what a hoot!

Punctuation

(Composed on 2 December 2011)

I often think;
about punctuation.
That controlling – authority which,
constructs. How we shall:
understand?
What is written –
and, a mere change.
In the punctuation
can affect the meaning;
drastically) or so I suppose.

Late at night the Great Spirit runs amuck in my brain

(Composed on 21 December 2011; I am grateful to Chris for suggesting the title for this rhyme)

A man with apache over one eye
Aztec me something but I don't know why.
"Mayan your business," I told him right out.
"I Comanche to stop," I wanted to shout.
"Incas you don't, they'll be repercussions":
that much I said, but only in Russian.
I had reservations, of course, for I knew
I had nootka to gain from speaking so plain.
I hopi that Yuma just understand
why it's my brain can get out of hand.
Dakota just put on the rack with my hat
is nothing to crow about but think of that:
end of the day we have nothing but words
that fly through our heads however absurd.

A tale of two kitties

(Completed on 31 December 2011; apologies to Charles Dickens)

There once were two kitties and each took a stance,
one lived in England, the other in France.
The times were the best, they were also the worst,
with political risks to both life and purse.
The kitty in England liked to eat fish,
the kitty in France preferred meat in her dish.
The kitty in England would go for a stroll
and then return home for some milk in her bowl.
The kitty in France would sit on the sill
and stared out the window until he looked ill.
The kitty in England was loyal to the king
and never would think of a disloyal thing.
But the kitty in France was rebellious at heart,
And was working to get an uprising to start.
But one day their owners crossed paths in Madrid,
and each felt excitement race through the id.
Soon they were lying together in bed,
their engines were roaring full steam ahead.
But what is important is what this would mean
for the kitties who want to clean and to preen.
Their owners decided to move in together
and settled in Spain because of the weather.
The kitties were ready, no need to pretend,
because they were quickly becoming dear friends.
And thus these two couples – people and cats –
abandoned their separate old habitats,
and moved in together to share joy and laughter
and lived ever merrily happy thereafter.

A gift of a rainbow (for Mutti)

(Composed on 2 July 2012)

I'll grab a piece of rainbow
and put it in a bag,
I'll give it to my mother:
I know that she'll be glad.
A rainbow shines and glows and shimmers,
lights up any space.
I'm already imagining
the smile across her face.

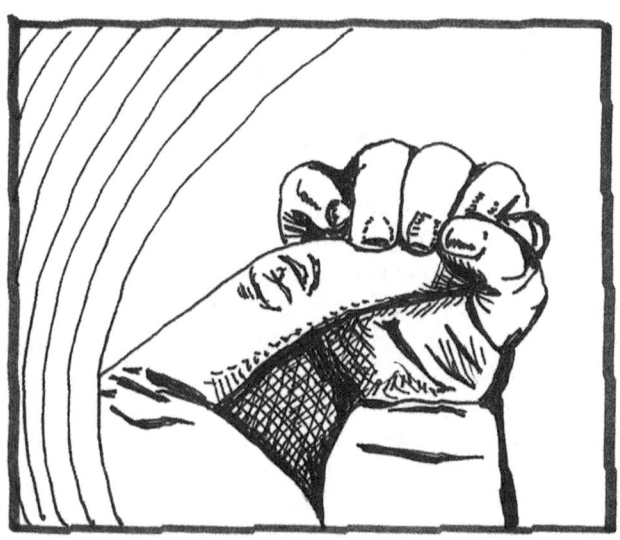

Thus spake Cecil

(Composed on 22 July 2011; revised on 17 October 2016. For all the Cecils in the world)

(Chorus)
"Load me in the cannon and light the fuse,
because there is no time to lose,
watch me soaring through the air
to fly to her for whom I care."
Thus spake Cecil, prophet and guard
who keeps close watch at the impound yard.

Cecil thinks of no one else save himself and Emma dear,
every time he hears her name, he breaks into a cheer.
He has "traveled" round the yard -- marching, strolling, skating --
but there's none who can compare with Emma, who's been waiting.
So now he says he's coming home, he's feeling light and heady,
he hopes that Emma will be there and that she's getting ready.

(Repeat chorus)

At the yard he impounds cars, and parks them in their lanes --
it is the kind of work he likes, so he can use his brains.
He thinks about the question if and when the cars need cleaning,
he thinks about the universe and its inner meaning.
He counts the cars three times a day to make sure none are missing,
then he thinks of Emma and dreams of future kissing.

(Repeat chorus)

On weekends when he has some time, he climbs up somewhere high,
he sets aside an hour or two just to prophesy.
He mostly thinks of future times for jolliness and fun,
and this is what he prophesies -- yes, that is how it's done.

His cat gave birth to kittens before her pussy-fix,
now his cat just sits at home beneath the crucifix.

(Repeat chorus)

Back in Trondheim Emma's gone to church to test the pews,
she thinks about her Cecil while she lights a fuse.
Her prophet Cecil doesn't want stigmata on his hands:
he has a huge collection of string and rubber bands.
Bur Emma wants to hear a bang and knows that C-4 works,
and now she waits a little while until she goes berserk.

Christopher Marlowe and his work

(Composed on 31 December 2012)

Chaucer didn't write his books – he's just some sort of faker –
No, old Chris Marlowe he did that, right after he wrote
Shakespeare.
Marlowe wrote the *Scarlet Letter*, also *Moby Dick*,
but other fellows take the credit: boy, it makes me sick.
That Gatsby book – that's Marlowe's work, and likewise *War and Peace*.
And *Don Quixote,* need you ask? Marlowe wrote it while in
Nice.
But Marlowe was so occupied with writing other people's
books,
he had no time to write his own,
though we too long mistook *Doc Faustus* for the work of
Marlowe,
but it wasn't so.
For Shakespeare wrote that book of his, though that was long
ago.
So now you have some sense of what you can learn in college,
and this is what we like to call truly special knowledge.

Department of Political Science & Psychology

Which is which?

World conquest through spoons

(Composed on 1 December 2010)

Are you up late at night worrying that old men will break into your house and steal your silverware?
Well...

The greybeards are coming
they're after your spoons,
I'm warning you now:
these greybeards are loons.
They're eager to confiscate
bottles and corks,
if you're not careful
they'll take all your forks.
The greybeards are coming
they're after your knives,
so grab your utensils
and run for your lives.
And don't be surprised
if they steal all your bowls,
you've got to be wondering:
what are their goals?
But think to yourself
how existence would look
if all the utensils
were held by these crooks.
They're building an empire,
we've got to move fast,
as long as our holdings
of spoons and forks last.

Derry down down down derry down

(Composed on 1 December 2010; inspired by George Stevens' 1775 song "What a court hath old England", to the melody of which this verse may be sung)

I'm worried that I may be coming in late,
I'm worried lest I arrive rather too soon,
I'm worried I may be too formal in dress,
And I'm worried I may be too casually dressed.
Derry down down down derry down,
Derry down down down derry down.

I'm worried the planet is getting too hot,
Maybe I'm ready but maybe I'm not,
I'm worried the planet is getting too cold
And I'm worried that all of my friends look so old.
Derry down down down derry down
Derry down down down derry down.

I'm worried that all of my friends look so young
I'm worried I might have a wart on my tongue,
I'm worried that some of my friends whom I've known
May worry too little or worry alone.
Derry down down down derry down
Derry down down down derry down.

I'm worried the rich control too much wealth,
I'm worried that worrying may harm my health,
It might have effects that are nasty and rough,
and I'm worried that I may not worry enough.
Derry down down down derry down,
Derry down down down derry down.

The promised land

(Composed on 13-14 December 2010; revised on 15 December 2010; modified on 14 August 2013)

I went to the other dimension,
I had some free time on my hands.
So I figured I might as well travel
to strange and unusual lands.
I'm sure NSA knows about it,
but naturally keeps it all mum,
they're probably terribly worried
that travelers there might succumb
to all the allures and attractions
that distracted me while I was there,
from paper clips made out of toffee
to popcorn that spread everywhere.
But the things that surprised me the most
were first that they didn't have guns
or weapons at all for that matter,
and that they were so fond of puns.
I don't know why it's been such a secret,
I wrote to the Congress about it:
the only reply I was given
maintained that dimension was crowded.
Too crowded for what I kept thinking,
but knew it was vain to inquire,
'cause maybe – this thought kept returning –
it was crowded with agents on hire
working for NSA's project
for defenses truly extensive:
but I would be ready to bet
that their project is much too expensive.
But when I recalled that my travel
that took me to other dimensions

showed no sign of NSA agents –
that tasked my impaired comprehension.
But maybe the government's lying,
and hasn't been there in the first place
and is telling us things that aren't true
our thinking thereby to erase.
As for me, I'm packing my luggage,
the other dimension looks grand.
I'm planning to settle there quickly,
could it be it's the new promised land?

John Bolton's dog

(Inspired by hearing presidential candidate John Bolton describe President Obama's speech about Libya as "a dog's breakfast"; composed on 31 March 2011)

John Bolton's dog likes breakfast and eats it every day,
but when it's time for breakfast, John Bolton's dog has needs.
She always orders bacon and fried eggs over easy,
and sometimes fried tomatoes and on this dish she feeds.

John Bolton's dog is ornery and snaps and growls and barks
at all the local passers-by, especially at the yuppies.
John Bolton's dog got pregnant by some mangy mutt,
and gave birth to a half a dozen mangy, toothy puppies.

John Bolton likes his doggie and takes her out on walks,
they wander through the public parks and growl at local ducks.
John Bolton hasn't named his dog, there's no name that quite fits,
Whenever someone thinks of one, John Bolton says it sucks.

John Bolton and his doggie don't have ticks or fleas:
the reason is they wash and dry with special kill-flea lotion.
What troubles them is hearing folk discuss the rights of unions,
or wanting higher minimum wage and raising a commotion.

John Bolton knows, as does his dog, that cyclists are scum:
people oughta drive in cars and get out on the freeway.
And when it comes to taxes, John Bolton truly feels
that rich folk earned what is their due and should enjoy some leeway.

And then when it's the evening, they watch the TV set,
the two of them pass judgment about what's good or foul.
And when some Jeffersonian espouses lib'ral prat,
John Bolton and his doggie will always start to growl.

Welcome in Libya

(Composed on 24 January 2011)

Welcome in Libya, heterosexual men
and attractive women under 35.
Please dress modestly,
remember that the Brother Leader
and King of Culture
loves you
and expects you to love him
in return.
Love means respect:
since you will love the Brother Leader,
you will show respect for him,
not criticize his rule
or his country
or his religion
or his tribe
or his family
or the Libyan media
or the Kufra oasis project.
Remember too:
there is no corruption in Libya,
only rewards for the deserving.
Would anyone deny
that the deserving deserve what they deserve?
Of course not!
Welcome in Libya!

Tired of the same old politics? Vote Bolshevik

(Composed on 11/12 March 2011. If you can't guess the tune, you're no Bolshevik!)

If you believe the rich should rule
and treat the citizens as dopes,
then, comrade, you are quite a fool
and you've given up all hope.
But the Bolsheviks are not the same
as the exploiters whom you know,
they light the revolution's flame
and then they make our spirits glow.
While the rich folks have stolen
from the workers and the tramps,
the Bolsheviks will change all this
and put the rich in camps.
If you're tired of the way
politicians have behaved,
then vote for Bolsheviks today --
you'll see: they're all the rave!

At the polls

(Composed on 12 April, for Torbjørn, who inspired this verse)

When I go to cast my vote, I want a dude what don't smell bad,
who's got no roaches in his hair, and one who's not entirely mad.
Important that his socks must match, his shirt should not be inside out.
I like it too that when he speaks he doesn't rave or scream or shout.
I don't much care if he can think or what his politics might be,
as long as how he's gonna vote won't bring harm to you or me.
I want a dude who walks to work or maybe sometimes takes the bus, a guy what's got a Maine Coon cat, about which pet he makes a fuss.
I'm gonna like it if he whistles, nice and low like a bassoon,
and even if it's just one note, I'm sure I'll hear a lovely tune.
But most important is this fact: he oughta wear a cowboy hat
and strut around in cowboy boots, inhabiting his habitat.

We are the illuminati

(Completed on 30 March 2011)

We are the illuminati: that's what you should call us, our mascot is the walrus.
We have secret meetings, where we make decisions, about our future missions.
We wear fancy bowties, and they always sparkle, especially in the darkle.
And if you ever were to ask us, what is our ambition, we'll say it's not perdition.
But people have illusions
about our aspirations,
and they reach conclusions,
and rich hallucinations.
We are the illuminati: that's what you should call us, our mascot is the walrus.
We have secret meetings, where we make decisions, about our future missions.
We wear fancy bowties, and they always sparkle, especially in the darkle.
And if you ever were to ask us, what is our ambition, we'll say it's not perdition.
What we like is dancing,
and leaping and some springing,
we do the Cucamonga,
and always like our singing.
And yes!! We are the illuminati: that's what you should call us, yes!

Bruno Bauer at Hippel's Pub

(Composed on 12 March 2011)

Bruno Bauer -- he liked kings
and he liked some other things.
He liked chatting with his friends
about the means to reach some ends.
At Hippel's pub he'd sit and drink
but held his nose before the stink
of other people's dumb ideas
but he promised he would free us
from th'oppression of free choice --
all the while he raised his voice.
He thought tsardom was divine,
he liked drinking riesling wine,
which he drank with bread and cheese --
before the tsar, fall to your knees.
There's no need to make decisions,
kings can make them -- with revisions.
With a tsar you'd never worry
and, of course, you won't feel sorry
'cause whatever might go wrong,
it's not your fault. Don't heed the throng
who say that kingship isn't right --
of course it is: it's built on might.

Who let the ants come in?

(Composed on 20 March 2011. Sing to the tune of "The E-R-I-E canal," a song written sometime in the 1800s by an unknown songster)

Oh, the ants smell something rotten,
their body odor's bad,
they also need some mouthwash but
they treat it like a fad.

(Hey) we had a swig of whiskey
and we had a round of gin,
but looking 'round we ask ourselves,
who let the ants come in?
who let the ants come in?

The chocolate donuts sprouted wings,
they're flying all around,
and sometimes donut crumbs fall down
to ants down on the ground.

(Hey) we had a swig of whiskey
and we had a round of gin,
but looking 'round we ask ourselves,
who let the ants come in?
who let the ants come in?

We see the lights go flicker,
the moon came in the door,
but looking down we see the ants
are marching 'cross the floor.

(Hey) we had a swig of whiskey
and we had a round of gin,
but looking 'round we ask ourselves,

who let the ants come in?
who let the ants come in?

The walls have started talking,
they say they want to dance,
but most of all they want to talk
about the local ants.

(Hey) we had a swig of whiskey
and we had a round of gin,
but looking 'round we ask ourselves,
who let the ants come in?
who let the ants come in?

The ants have got it very rough,
at least from what I've seen:
four hundred males per colony
for just a single queen.

(Hey) we had a swig of whiskey
and we had a round of gin,
but looking 'round we ask ourselves,
who let the ants come in?
who let the ants come in?

So far it's humans who have ruled
-- and you've seen what that's worth,
but maybe it's the time to make
ants masters of the earth,
and looking 'round we ask ourselves,
who let the ants come in,
who let the ants come in?

Inky Dinky Baby Doc

(Composed on 24 January 2011; if you don't recognize which melody inspired this verse, you may wish to brush up on British songs from World War One)

Duvalier from Haiti was Papa Doc
Duvalier was hated as Papa Doc
Duvalier, the ruling boss, hadn't been kissed in forty years
Inky Dinky Papa Doc!

He'd fought disease and won acclaim: Papa Doc.
Then he tried another game -- Papa Doc,
he was elected president but used some voodoo on his folk,
Inky Dinky Papa Doc!

He said he was a houngan priest, Papa Doc.
But the peasants -- they were fleeced, Papa Doc,
He stay in power 'til he died, but none of his people even cried,
Inky Dinky Papa Doc!

Upon his death his son came in: Baby Doc.
Is it true he lived in sin? Baby Doc,
He lived in style and soon got rich but left his people in the ditch,
Inky Dinky Baby Doc!

When Haitians died he sold their parts: Baby Doc.
He spent all day consuming tarts, Baby Doc.
When he wed he spent a mint, served as chief for quite a stint,
Inky Dinky Baby Doc!

But Haitians thought his rule was rough: Baby Doc.
Eventually they'd had enough, Baby Doc.
The people rose, the leader froze, they threw him out upon his toes,
Inky Dinky Baby Doc
Once again, and
Inky Dinky Baby, Inky Dinky Baby, Inky Dinky Baby Doc.

I approve of this message

(Composed on 19 December 2010)

Senator Phlenator sleeps with a hog,
his thinking's unclear and he's lost in a fog,
he's stolen your money and swindled his mom,
for his own reasons he's planting a bomb
under the Library of Congress's books:
this is god-awful, just see how it looks.
His thinking on terrorists? Well, you can bet
he doesn't consider them much of a threat,
he likes to waste money, thinks taxes should climb,
his friends are engaged all in high-collar crime.
He takes lots of bribes, breaks all his chairs,
makes his ten children eat nothing but pears.
The incumbent senator is such a slob,
isn't it time that he loses his job?

I'm Candidate Bandittate, and I approve of this message.

Forward, brothers!

(Composed on 29 July 2011)

Forward, brothers! We will win:
if we don't, we'll lose ag'in.
Everyone should think like us,
if they don't, we'll make a fuss.
We'll commit mass suicide
if the people won't decide
that we brothers know what's right:
Right is right, and might makes might.

Department of Pre-Law Studies

"A jury consists of twelve persons chosen to decide who has the better lawyer." -- Robert Frost

Jail the poor, or Ode to Judge Fudge

(Composed on 14 January 2011)

"What if we should have a problem,
like an earthquake or a flood?
Masses of dishevelled people
might decide to spill some blood,"
so said Judge -- His Honor -- Fudge,
a man renowned for knowing much.
But when he shouted "Jail the poor!"
some wondered if he'd lost his touch.
"Jail the poor," he shouted out,
"let the news be sent about."

"Best to be a little cautious,
get the riff-raff of the streets,"
mouthed His Honor in the mirror,
"they're capable of many feats."
He was smartest of the judges,
kept his eyeball on his goal,
therefore they should heed his warning:
lock up thieves before they stole.
"Jail the poor," he shouted out,
"let the news be sent about."

He was master of acoustics --
if he hit a certain pitch,
he was sure he'd levitate
and leave his colleagues in the ditch.
"When I'm soaring ever upwards,
and I'm getting very high,
you'll be seeing me above you,
soaring 'cross the evening sky."

"Jail the poor," he shouted out,
"let the news be sent about."

When I think of Judge J. Fudge I
often wonder what he's doing,
now that he must be retired or
is there something else he's brewing?
Once I sent his name to TIME
and I told them loud and clear:
Here's a judge you should consider
for your cover -- Man of the Year!
"Jail the poor," he shouted out,
"let the news be sent about."

Let us define

(*Composed on 30 January 2011*)

Let us define marriage:

There must be two people, now that is for sure,
it just wouldn't do with one or yet fewer.
Should we then say they can be immature?
No, surely it's best they be wise and mature.
Ther're few who are wise or mature at age twenty,
but once they reach forty, of wisdom there's plenty.
Of course, there are none who would want to define
a marriage as following some grand design
that partners should speak without knowledge of grammar
or involve a recividist, liar, or shammer.
Nor should we require that it be without pets
or that the poor couple abstain from baguettes.
But if all of these limits would make the thing worse,
then logic dictates that we choose the reverse.

And accordingly,
It is logical to define a marriage as the union of two honest adults age forty or older, without criminal records, who speak flawless, grammatically correct sentences, have at least one pet, chosen from an approved list of animals, and eat baguettes. No baguettes, no marriage.

Three men in Evanston

(Inspired by an article in The Daily Northwestern, 27 January 2011, p. 1, reporting that "the controversial 'brothel law'...prohibits three unrelated people from living in the same house." Composed on 3 February 2011. May be sung to the tune of Verdi's "La donna è mobile")

Three men in Evanston
all above ninety years,
decided to share a flat,
but look how it appears:
under the standing law,
three unrelated gents,
living together thus
must be collecting rents.

It is a brothel,
even with these fossils,
the law declares it
and so it is.
And so it is.
A bro-o-o-o-thel!

One night police arrived
these gents were quite surprised,
"What are you running here?
Brothel!" the cops surmised.
There were no customers,
there were no ladies there,
they were all past their prime,
had not collected fare.

It is a brothel,
even with these fossils,
the law declares it
and so it is.
And so it is.
A bro-o-o-o-thel!

"Brothels are not allowed.
You must come down to jail,
where you'll be registered:
Please don't tell us you're frail.
This is a question of
what the law says it is:
and by a brothel is
meant what you have here.

It is a brothel,
even with you fossils,
the law declares it
and so it is.
And so it is.
A bro-o-o-o-thel!

It is a brothel,
even with these fossils,
the law declares it
and so it is.
And so it is.
A bro-o-o-o-thel!

The case of the moldy cheese

(Begun on 8 August 2011, completed on
3 December 2011)

Detective Chief Inspector Gall is ready to investigate,
he always comes – yes – right on time, he's never early, never late.
One fine day as he was resting, Detective Chief Inspector Gall
put his pencil on the desk, responding to an urgent call.
There was someone in distress, who needed some assistance please:
it seems there'd been some sabotage and there was fungus on the cheese.
Detective Chief Inspector Gall hurried to the factory,
the truth was most elusive, everything refractory.
He talked to all the workers there and this is what the Chief was told:
There'd been some trouble at the plant with this result that there was mold!
This was a frightful, serious matter – surely there could be no doubt.
Detective Chief Inspector Gall would make sure that he found it out,
who had done the sabotage and caused so much unease
by introducing fungus mold in such a crate of cheese.
One hundred five employees were working at the plant,
of evidence no not a shred, evidence was scant.
But was the cheese a camembert, a tilsit, or a cheddar?
identify the victim first and see if it's a spreader.
Once he could identify the nature of the cheese,
he'd figure out the motive with celerity and ease.
But lo! It was Gloucester, and even yes a Double:
now he knew the case was mean and packed a lot of trouble.
The motive to attack a Double Gloucester crate of cheese
meant that this was someone who would not be charging fees
to make a fresh delivery precisely of this crate
and with this the list of suspects was reduced to eighty-eight.

But four of these were English and let me underscore
that this reduced the suspect list to only eighty-four.
But sixty-four of them maintained they loved the cheese aplenty,
and if he could believe them then the list was pared to twenty.
So now he asked the lot of them to raise their hands aloft,
so he could see which hands were rough and which of them
were soft.
But all of them had silky skin, their fingernails were clean
except that nine of them had fungus in-between.
So now the Chief Inspector declared he'd solved the case:
this was a grand conspiracy, execrable and base.
All nine men were guilty, they'd hatched their little plot
and thought that there was no one who would apprehend the lot.
The paddy wagon soon arrived, the nine were put in cuffs,
and as the siren blared success, they shouted "Give us puffs!"

The Perfect Murder

(Composed on 9 June 2013)

A murder in the kitchen, a body on the floor --
how absolutely horrid, be quick and close the door.
It would have been much better if the deed' been done
somewhere in the living room -- and there, a smoking gun.
'Cause living rooms are suited for grisly things galore
but just hang on a moment and I will tell you more.
The shooting of the victim with bullets through the heart
shows contempt for human life and disregard for art.
Much better with a large harpoon, a halberd, or a spear:
these would be marks of someone with murder as career.
And so much blood was splattered and even on the chairs,
cupboards broken into bits, in need of some repairs.
But any good professional leaves furniture intact
and cleans up any messes: (and) that is just a fact.
No note of any kind was left and that is simply rude.
At least the killer might have left some greetings, nothing crude.
A little note might let police believe they have a clue
but that's not necessarily anything that's true.
And so you see this murder was carried out quite wrong,
a proper killer would have known it doesn't take so long
to leave the house in order and clean up blood and mess,
to write a friendly little note in which he could confess.
Yes, that's how murders should be done, if they're done at all:
be courteous and tidy up, or folk might be appalled.

Department of Slavic Studies

Yes, we have an entire department devoted to this subject. You don't believe us? Well, why would we lie?

Rus from Florida

(Composed on 6 August 2010)

He's a burly chillavyek
and he smokes those cheap papirosi,
he's so rich, he's "bogat" –
that's what they call it in St. Petersburg,
Florida.
His name is Rus,
it's short for Ivan,
but you can call him Boris,
I call him Vlad
just to annoy him.
When he goes for a walk
he takes his sabaka along,
his sabaka barks at the lyudi
on the mall.
But Rus-Ivan-Boris-Vlad
stands tall,
smoking his papirosis.

A girl named Lapuca

(Composed on 6 March 2011)

There once was a girl named Lapuca,
who liked Bach's Toccata and Fuca,
which she played on the flute
with a toodle-dee-toot:
you'd like it, just come take a looka.

There once was a fellow named Biktor,
whose pet was a boa constrictor.
His snake lived on maco,
and smoked some tobacco,
and was a convincing evictor.

There once was a pectopah rated
the best in the gopod and slated
to host inostransi
in skirts or in pantsi,
who wanted to dine and be feted.

There once was a postman named Bopic
who never gave up to be hopik
that one day he'd team
with the girl of his dream,
and together they'd then dance the gopak.

My cat can hum

(Composed 19/21 February 2011)

My cat can hum a tune or too -- indeed that is his job.
He likes to hum old wartime songs especially 'bout the NOB.
He hums the strident marches that Comrade Tito's troops
were marching to in time of war, he hums about the MUPs.
And when it comes to Yugo songs, my cat is such a wiz --
and even hums a workers' song about a local SIZ.
But all those things have come and gone, belong to ancient "lore",
and knowing this he also hums a tune about the OHR.

Department of Zoology

We study insects too.

My goldfish are all Nazis

(Composed on 13-14 August 2010)

My goldfish are all Nazis –
of that I am quite sure –
and though I've tried a dozen times
so far I've found no cure.
They swim in tight formation,
up and down they file,
they're sticking out their little fins
as if to say "Sieg Heil!"
Their fish tank has some sea weed,
some colored pebbles too;
a little sign marks "Poland"
in letters red and blue.
The fish have lots of sunlight,
while Poland's in the shade,
but all of their activity
might mean they will invade.
But goldfish plans – what might they be
for all these colored rocks?
I think their brains are pretty small,
they are no mental jocks.
So maybe I'll not start to fret
if goldfish plans are set,
I may not know what they have planned
to do with all their sand,
but what's the worst that they can do?
Don't tell me 'til they're through,
I just don't want to contemplate,
what goldfish can create.

Of penguins and field mice

(Composed on 31 March 2011)

Some of my best friends are penguins,
at least I think they're penguins.
Of course, they might be field mice
disguised as penguins –
how would I know the difference?
Have you ever seen a field mouse
disguised as a penguin?
If so, you know it can be hard to tell;
if not, then you are no authority
on whether a field mouse
can pass as a penguin.

Guard goose

(Composed on 11 and 18 November 2010)

I have a goose
that's on the loose,
she's keeping guard
of house and yard,
and on our walks
she always squawks
at every passerby.

Sally the goose
takes no abuse,
she will confide
she can't abide
a singing frog,
a warbling hog,
or anything loud at all.

If you could read
my goose's mind,
you would discern
the ties that bind
Sally the goose
to duty's call.
A guard goose she is – that's all!

Sex-crazed dolphins

(Composed on 19 November 2010)

Sex-crazed dolphins –they stay trim
exercising while they swim.
They're always naked, I suppose –
they disdain any kind of clothes.
They don't wear scarves around their necks,
they're always thinking they want sex.
Sex-crazed dolphins in the sea,
loving life and swimming free.

I have seen them swim in packs,
they're just wanting to relax,
dolphins looking for a place to dock,
it's orgy time on dolphins' clock,
but after they go on for hours,
it's time for them to take their showers.
Is this news or had you guessed
how these dolphins find their rest?

Pussycat junction

(Composed on 24 November 2010)

At pussycat junction every cat
comes around to have a chat,
they boast about the birds they've caught
and talk about the scraps they've fought.
Kit-kats like to purchase stuff
and they like to brag and bluff,
buying things they do not need:
is this folly? Is this greed?
Fancy collars, woolly shawls –
who's the cutest cat of all?
Kit-kat's food dish made of gold,
all things new and nothing old.

If the mayor were a pigeon

(Composed on 17 February 2011)

If the mayor were a pigeon, there is much that he could do
like make some wise decisions about the public loo.
Why build a lot of toilets, thus fostering enslavement
to sitting on the toilet seat when there's space right on the pavement?
If people would just realise, as pigeons surely do,
how vastly more convenient and more efficient too,
it is to simply find relief the moment that you feel
the slightest urge in that regard, they'd ape the birds with zeal.
And think about the meals we eat, with plates and forks and knives,
and all the soap and water used to wash them through our lives.
But pigeons -- glad you asked me -- dine right on the street,
they don't use knives or forks or plates and yet they keep quite neat.
They never wash the dishes or purchase cups or plates,
they never go on diets, 'cause they never watch their weights.
They use the public fountain to give themselves a bath,
the water's fine, come jump right in -- hey, you can do the math.
You'll never have to clean the tub or stock your shelf with soap.
So when election time arrives, the pigeon wants your vote.

Each squirrel is unique

(Composed on 21 February 2011)

You might think squirrels look just quite the same
and be entirely disinclined to call each by her name,
but if you look more closely, then I do suppose
that you might find some differences in eyes and teeth and nose.
Some of them are beautiful, some are merely pretty,
but each of them deserves her own unique and special ditty.
And surely if you want to have from other species friends,
then treat them not as merely means but all of them as ends.

My cuddle-y cat

(Composed on 7 September 2010)

My cat is very cuddle-y
he fell into a puddle-y
and now he is all muddle-y
and feeling quite befuddle-y.

My fish needs a haircut

(Composed on 22 November 2010)

Whenever my fish
needs his scales shined and polished
I pick him right out of the tank,
I drive him downtown
in my new SUV
with him sitting right at my flank.
Most barbers will cater
to humans alone,
but some will assist with your pets.
So bring in your lizard,
your frog or your toad,
your goldfish will get what it gets:
massage for his gils,
and tweaking his fins,
and scraping the moss off his tongue.
With service like this,
you won't be surprised
that your fish will forever be young.

The bamboo tree

(Composed on 21 October 2010)

Many are the insects you can see
only have to climb the bamboo tree
climbing to the top you see them all
dontcha think that they are all in thrall?
Elephants and donkeys don't say "moo",
they're safest when they're in the zoo,
All of our solutions – it's quite plain –
show we have malfunctions in the brain.
Th'problem is we live in here and now,
we cannot see past the barnyard cow.
There's gotta be an animal that can know
what's in the direction where we go.

Every fish is a saint

(Composed on 5 August 2011)

I have an acquarium, seventeen fish,
they're all very pleased with my satellite dish.
They like to watch comedies, crime shows as well
and look very happy around their sea shells.
The first four I named -- Matthew, Mark, Luke and John --
are handsome and like to be waited upon.
And then there're the others: Andrew and James,
Peter, Matthias -- remember their names --
Bartholemew, Philip, Simon, and Judas,
but which of my fish do you think is the rudest?
Surely not Little James, Big John, or Jude
and Thomas the Doubter is, no, never rude.
There's just one remaining: that's Devon Delight!
But Devon's unsullied and always polite,
in fact, I must say, all my fish have good manners,
you won't hear them shouting or grabbing for banners.
You won't see them shoving or needing restraint,
oh no, every fish in my tank is a saint.

Animalosity

(*Composed on 10 November 2011*)

Do cuckoos spit and, if they do,
do you think they'd spit at you?
Might a cockroach take a stroll?
Does a cockroach have a soul?
A worm can wiggle for a mile,
but have you ever seen one smile?

The fly

(Composed on 10 November 2011)

The fly needs lots of exercise:
it's flying all around.
It zooms up to the ceiling
and swoops down to the ground.
It climbs up on the window
and goes just any place.
But most of all it likes to land
right upon my face.
I help it get its exercise
by waving far and wide.
I think the fly appreciates
that I am on its side.
And when it's time to go to sleep
and lie down on my bed,
the little fly – it joins me,
and rests upon my head.

Save the planet

(Composed on 20 November 2011)

I'm ridin' up the elevator
with the new interrogator,
asks me questions 'bout my gator,
don't know where I should begin.

I try to tell him with a smile
that it's just a crocodile
on my rooftop on the tiles:
comes to gators, count me in.

Then come teams of fumigators,
cockroach clan eliminators:
don't they know insectorgators
have a right to life?

Chop the trees and clear the jungle:
that's much more than just a bungle,
turns the planet into dungle.
Save the planet, peace not strife!

I love the wildlife

(Composed in Tartu, on 22 May 2012)

I love the wildlife, mosquitoes included,
especially the fat one whose bottom's protruded
into my nose and under my clothes.

I love the wildlife and – yes – that means ants,
especially the ones that crawl inside my pants.
They march and keep beat, and crawl onto my feet.

I love the wildlife – now here's a surprise:
I open my doors to all manner of flies,
their legs covered in fuzz. Let them come in and buzz.

I love the wildlife, and insects are best,
What mascot is seen on my family crest?

Halibut

(Composed on 17 July 2012; for Mikhail)

A halibut will, a halibut will, a halibut will not lie,
whatever you ask of a halibut, the fish will never lie.

There is a man on Brixton Street with halibuts as pets,
he claims that he is happy with the company he gets
from talking to his halibuts – they never contradict
or start to talk back when the man becomes a little strict.
He often asks them questions just in case they know
the answer to a question, or can play the piccolo.
But in his long experience, his fishes never lied
or claimed to play some instruments which they have never tried.

A halibut will, a halibut will, a halibut will not lie,
whatever you ask of a halibut, the fish will never lie.

And down on Pilson-Pilson Road you'll find a baroness
and if you ask her nicely, you'll find she will profess
that all her fourteen halibuts have much respect for truth,
although she has confessed to me they're still in early youth.
But like the man on Brixton Street, if she asks a question
of her fish she knows the answer's fit for her ingestion –
not that they have answered even once despite her tries,
but their continued silence means at least they never lie.

A halibut will, a halibut will, a halibut will not lie,
whatever you ask of a halibut, the fish will never lie.

President Minah

(Composed on 8—9 December 2012; revised on 18 December 2012)

If a minah bird were president, you know he'd just repeat
whatever he had heard that day around or on the street.
When minah birds hear wisdom, they sound so very wise,
it's true I tell you, every word, just open up your eyes.
If a minah bird were president, we'd only need to see
that senseless talk's excluded where the president will be.
So let a minister intone, "Our country favors peace,"
and that's the message that our bird will speedily release.
And if another minister says "People want to work,"
then that is what the bird will say before it goes berserk.
But best of all with minah birds, there isn't one that's mad –
they may not be original, but there's none that we'd call bad.

When the bird's on his toes, here's how it goes:

"Mr. President, there's something we need to discuss."
"Squawk! We need to discuss, we need to discuss."
"There are problems in the Middle East and in the defense
department, people want to know if we intend to go to war."
"Squawk! Go to war, go to war."
"Meanwhile, at home, the economy's rocky. Many people
have lost their jobs and want to go back to work."
"Squawk! Back to work, back to work."
"And then there's the question, should we raise the taxes?"
"Squawk! Raise the taxes, raise the taxes."
"And finally, Mr. President, we all want to know whether you
plan to seek a second term."
"Squawk! Second term, second term."

Bad breath in dogs

(Composed on 31 October 2012)

My dog's breath is fragrant, like roses in spring –
come, give him a kiss, and you'll never forget it!
Draw close to my dog, inhaling deeply,
I am quite sure that you'll never regret it.
Your dog, however, has terrible breath,
it's really as if he's been feeding on trash.
What do you feed him that he smells so bad –
a mixture of cigarettes, mushrooms, and mash?

Top sirloin is best if you value your dog,
sprinkle rose petals on top of his meat.
Then, as he eats it, his breath will improve
and soon all your neighbors will think it a treat
to sit by your dog and inhale his breath:
you might just discover you've launched a new fad.
But bad breath in dogs can only be said
to be noxious and nasty and just downright bad.

Do you believe in goats?

(Composed on 12 May 2018)

Simon Pieman's brothers – they don't believe in goats:
you see, they've never seen a goat, so why become believers?
They laugh at anyone who claims that she has seen a goat,
they tell themselves this is the product of a raging fever.
They also don't believe there's life on any other planets:
until they've seen it for themselves, they'd rather not agree,
since why accept that things exist, until you pay a visit,
and verify that there are creatures there for you to see.
Ghosts, well that is different! 'cause that means haunted houses –
the brothers aren't conformists, they say in perfect diction.
So they insist that ghosts and demons really don't exist,
and ghosts, like UFOs and goats, are simply works of fiction.

The mystery of feline reproduction

(composed 19-20 May 2018)

All cats are female,
all dogs are male,
snails have no gender,
snakes are all tail.
Dogs like their kitties,
and here comes a litter --
small hybrid puppies:
they couldn't look fitter.
In a town without dogs
you'll never find kittens:
that's just a matter of history.
Now that you understand
how this is done,
there is no longer a mystery.

Department of History

"[T]here are known knowns; there are things we know we know.
We also know there are known unknowns; that is to say we know there are some things we do not know.
But there are also unknown unknowns — the ones we don't know we don't know." –
Donald Rumsfeld
Here in the Department of History we want to know both what we know and what we don't know.

Hey, Martin van Buren

(Composed on 10—12 December 2010; sing to the tune of Tex Ritter's "Rye Whiskey", which he performed in the film, "Song of the Gringo," 1936)

Oh Martin van Buren was once at the top,
he danced the quadrille 'til his partners would drop.
Among all our presidents, he danced the best,
and never but never but never would rest.
Hey, Martin van Buren, you were quite a guy,
but now you have claimed your reward in the sky.
Ooh-wooh-wooh, ooh-wooh-wooh, ooh-wooh-wooh, oo-ooh wooh ha!
Yip, yip, woop la!

Some people will ask you, what good did you do?
Jess tell 'em that you did no damage – that's true.
You served in the White House for four years in all,
and showed off your two-step at the ole White House ball.
Hey, Martin van Buren, you were quite a guy,
but now you have claimed your reward in the sky.
Ooh-wa-wa, ooh-wa-wa, ooh-hoo, ooh-hoo wooh ha!
Yip, yip, woop la!

I've heard that the sarabande is quite complex
for members and nonmembers of either sex.
But you mastered it totally, you were quite adept,
while as dancers the senators were quite inept.
Hey, Martin van Buren, you were quite a guy,
but now you have claimed your reward in the sky.
Ooh-wooh-wooh, ooh-wooh-wooh, ooh-wooh-wooh, oo-ooh wooh ha!
Yip, yip, woop la!

You were dancin', van Buren, with vigor and style,
and for every young maiden you flashed your sweet smile.
You danced with panache and such elegant flair,
you had no competition 'til Mr. Astaire.
And hey, Martin van Buren, you were quite a guy,
but now you have claimed your reward in the sky.
Ooh-wooh-wooh, ooh-wooh-wooh, ooh-wooh-wooh, oo-ooh wooh ha!
Yip, yip, woop la!

The King is Mad

(Started on 15 December, finished on 25 December 2010)

After a pleasing midday repast,
King George the Third fancied an outing.
Although he had lost his lands in the West,
he had finally finished his pouting.
He clapped his hands twice and then shouted out,
"So let us be off, merry men.
Harness the horses and polish the carriage,
we'll drive to a close forest glen."

And so they took off with a rattley boom
and drove down a gravely road,
they passed an Old Hickory tree and a fence
and passed a small Mill House – we make no pretense.
An American sphinx they passed on the left,
a tippy canoe was tipped on the right.
They spied a red fox in wide field of poppies,
as a Kansas cyclone brought every delight.

King George, his royal personage, chatted away
to no one at all, but was feeling so cheery.
Then they came to a forest glen, barely in time,
for the horses were getting quite weary.
The King looked around, his eyes growing wide,
jumped out of the carriage and ran to a tree,
exclaiming quite joyfully, tipping his crown,
"Hey, Louis, you rotter, it's Georgie, it's me!"

Yes, Louis the Sixteenth was clearly in view,
just standing alone in the clime.
They could hear the soundtrack music so sweet,

as befitted two kings in their prime.
They chatted so amiably as two kings can do,
and exchanged many a joke,
but his driver and staff looked on quite aghast,
as the king conversed with an oak.

"King Louis" said:
"Faith is like a sparrow
that flies around for miles,
looking for a rooftop
to rest upon its tiles.
It flits around from place to place
and sometimes it is certain
that it has found just what it sought
like good old Thomas Merton."

To which, King George replied:
"I'm standing in a pudding,
a weasel is my cook.
I once sprang up a chimney
just to have a look.
But there was nothing much to see,
and so I went back down,
grabbed my scepter, donned my crown,
dressed up once more in royal gown."

But it was not King Louis at all, nor a fat imposter,
nor even mother or his dad,
but only an oak tree full with verdant leaves.
Yes, truly the king had gone mad –
yet, wise in his madness and mad in his wisdom:
some said he was even insane.
But we should be discreet and a little genteel,
for his majesty had a long reign.

Ponce de Leon and the Fountain of Youth

(Composed 21/23 December 2010)

For many a year, old Ponce did hear
of amazing miraculous cures.
He'd leave old age behind, if he could just find
the fountain of youth – he was sure.

He looked all around – on the hills, on the ground,
under each three-leaf clover,
on the mountainous slopes – preserving his hopes:
he really did search all over.

He hiked many a mile, such was his style,
dreaming again and again
how he'd sip from the cup – no, he'd never give up!
All the while he intoned this refrain:

"The older I'll get, the younger I'll get,
when I get to be ninety, I'll look like I'm ten.
When I turn hundred twelve, I'll be newborn once more,
and then I can start life all over again."

But Pone de Leon never did find
this fountain of youth and of cheer,
and today we remember him only as he
who wasted so many a year.

The Seven Cities of Cibola

(Composed on 21 December 2010)

The Spaniard Coronado
was out in Colorado,
he was seeking Eldorado
but did not have luck.

So he talked to the locals,
while wearing bifocals,
they were no yokels
and offered to help.

"If it's gold you needola,
then go to Cibola,
this is no fibula,"
and that's what they said.

"There are seven cities,
but it's such a pity
that the roads are so gritty,
but it's worth the trip."

So, based on this rumor,
and perhaps a brain tumor –
in his helmet, a plumer –
he set out to find

streets that were golden
with silver half molten,
he felt so emboldened
but still had no luck.

Now you might be guessin'
what could be the lesson –
it's this: don't be messin'
in lands that aren't yours!

You cannot be right against the party, or Trotsky agreed with himself

(Composed on 27—28 August 2010)

It's clear that if the party's right
and you don't agree
that you are clearly in the wrong
and don't think that you're free,
'cause freedom means that you are right
and not to be in error,
to choose to stay in ignorance
is self-inflicted terror.
You cannot be right
you cannot be right
against the party, no!

This insight came from Trotsky,
before he lost to Koba,
At least he didn't lose his teeth,
for that he thanked his zubar.
But once he'd lost to Stalin
ole Trotsky said the key
would be to make another party
with which he could agree.
You cannot be right
you cannot be right
against the party, no!

An International was what
was needed all around,
it would be number 4 because
the Third had run aground.
And if he ran the party, well,
he knew he would agree

with everything the party said,
the slogan would still be:
You cannot be right
you cannot be right
against the party, no!

Ode to Jefferson's wheel of cheese

(Inspired by a real event in Thomas Jefferson's life, and composed on 8 February 2011)

The Baptists of Cheshire,
they took the measure
of what they thought Jefferson wanted the most.
A wheel of fromage
would be no mirage –
at twelve hundred pounds it would be quite the toast
of people of taste
who never would waste
the chance to be dining on cheese through the night.
He'd offer to serve
full cheese hors d'oeuvres
whenever he had guests he wished to invite.
The sweet smell of cheese
was blown in the breeze
both inside the White House and out on the grounds,
and when he was done
and James Madison
took over he found there was still cheese around.

How did he choose?

(Composed on 9 January 2011. Inspired by certain events during the War of 1812, as well as by the 1961 song "Et maintenant" / "What now my love," music by Gilbert Becaud and original French lyrics by Pierre Delanoe; after the huge international success of the song, English lyrics were provided by Carl Sigman)

In 1812, the US felt cocky,
thought it could take some of Britain's land.
So war was launched, but it was rocky,
Detroit soon fell into Britain's hand.

General Hull threw in the towel,
but started to mull, just what to do.
For a white flag, he had a clean towel
but also a soiled one, that smelled so foul.

How did he choose? What would it mean
if he should hoist a towel too clean?
How could he lose, when he'd felt stronger?
But that did not matter any longer.

What mattered now was how to surrender
and somehow that was a real mind bender.
General Hull knew that what mattered
was keeping his cool, when his force was tattered.

General Hull, who can forget
how you decided, when you were upset?
I think that you chose the one that was soiled,
because all your men had fought and toiled.
Bye bye.

The channeling Olympics

(Composed on 22 November 2010; revised on 29 November 2010: may be sung to the tune of "The Hunters of Kentucky," 1821, a song in turn set to the tune of "Miss Bailey's Ghost," which has been credited to George Colman the elder, 1732—1794, and George Colman the younger, 1762—1836)

Hey Olympics
the channeling Olympics
hey Olympics
the channeling Olympics.

There was a famous medium,
he joined the competition:
he channeled old man Aaron Burr
who'd been charged with sedition,
and Aaron Burr, what did he say?
He openly deniyed
That he was guilty in the least –
he claimed that he was friyed.

Hey Olympics
the channeling Olympics
hey Olympics
the channeling Olympics.

Another fellow boasted then
that he could channel royalty,
and quickly summoned Bonnie Prince,
accused him of disloyalty,
but Charlie wasn't satisfied
with life's continued tedium,
and most of all rejected
all the charges from this medium.
Hey Olympics
the channeling Olympics
hey Olympics
the channeling Olympics.

Napoleon, yes Bonaparte
was channeled by another,
but wouldn't talk of anything
except his dear old mother.
We'd really hoped to hear him tell
of some important battle,
but yet instead of hearing that,
we listened to his prattle.

Hey Olympics
the channeling Olympics
hey Olympics
the channeling Olympics.

A fourth contestant came to bat
with Babe Ruth on his channel,
he wiped the breadcrumbs from his brow
with half a dampened flannel.
He asked the Babe if he could hit
a hundred in a season,
but Babe Ruth said he couldn't see
whatever was the reason.

Hey Olympics
the channeling Olympics
hey Olympics
the channeling Olympics.

Well hello, Zhivkov

(May be sung to the tune of "Hello Dolly"; composed on 6 and 9 September 2010)

Well hello, Zhivkov,
it's so nice, Zhivkov,
to see the posters with your smiling face.
You're looking wise, Zhivkov,
and your eyes, Zhivkov,
follow me as I go to another place.
Well yes, you know, Zhivkov,
where we go, Zhivkov,
in meeting all our goals within the plan!
So, Comrade Zhivkov, you are
such a supernova,
count me as your most obedient fan!

Well well, hello, Comrade,
lucky us, Comrade,
that all your children are so bright and strong,
you gave them posts, Zhivkov,
it's them I toast, Zhivkov,
it's nice to have you back where you belong (with us).
You changed the names, Comrade,
of men and dames, Comrade,
to sound more Slavic than they were before,
So – Comrade, you've always been a star,
Comrade, you've always been a star,
Comrade, you've always been a shining star.

Why did Arthur?

(Composed on 6 October 2010)

Why did Arthur, King of Celts,
whose knights all wore bright crimson belts,
hope to find the Holy Grail
hidden in an English vale?
Why did he receive his sword
from a hand from in the fjord?
Why was Merlin such a wiz
that he could make the river fizz?
And why was round a better shape
for the table where they ate?

Skiing with Karadžić

(Inspired by a news report published during the Bosnian war, 1992-95, that Bosnian Serbs had opened a ski resort near the frontlines and that skiers there could hear the sounds of the fighting in the distance. Composed on 11/12 February 2011)

There may be war down in the valley
but here in Pale you can ski.
We are winning, check the tally,
in the RS Serbs are free.
In the distance folk are fleeing,
some of them may lose their scalps.
Here in Pale we are skiing,
high in Bosnia's cherished alps.
As you ski down snowy slopes,
cock your ears, you hardly hear
sounds of battle in the distance,
just keep skiiing, tourist-dear.
Where the mountain goats once grazed,
we have smoothed the rocks away.
Take your hats off, be amazed:
join us now – make no delay.
Skiing near the conflict zone –
this is something quite unique.
Here you'll never feel alone:
try Karadžić's skiing week.

Trotsky's rabbits

(Composed on 18 November 2010)

Trotsky had some rabbits
he kept in a pen,
they had such tempered habits
that he always said of them:
"These, my rabbits,
they're loyal and true,
they'd never cater
to Stalin's brew."

The rabbits had a system
to meet each rabbit's needs:
decisions in committees
allocating feeds.
The rabbits had
self-management –
firm foundation
like cement.

When it came to irrigation,
it should be permanent –
so said all Trotsky's rabbits
and that is what they meant.
His rabbits knew
to get good crops
you've got to irrigate
the land a lot.

So the cry went out
from Trotsky's rabbits:
"Permanent irritation
and tempered habits!

and when we prey on lettuce
and lettuce is our prey,
we often like to sing and say –
time for dinner, lettuce prey!"

War or peace? We're still laughing

(Inspired by reading about Serbia during World War Two, and, yes, Žanka was a real person. Composed on 17 February 2011)

Hail Nedić, our prince of light and lightness!
He knows it is good to laugh, to feel the brightness.
Yes, our heroes are at the front, giving their blood,
they fight the communists in the forests and in the mud.
But in Belgrade, we have peace or something like peace,
even though the struggle for our unity will never cease.
Some apartments have become vacant and at the camps,
they are hiring guards to keep guard and fix the clamps
on the inmates. We put some of them in a hutch.
But at the theater, in the evenings, I laugh so much,
some of the actors' lines are so funny,
I laugh so hard my nose gets runny.
Žanka, you make me laugh – you bring me something like bliss, too,
and I think to myself, maybe I want to kiss you.
Here in the cities, we love our comedic artisans,
but out in the forests, our brave men are fighting the Partisans.
Yes, these are heavy times, when the future is being decided,
and our nation, led by General Nedić, is being joyfully guided
forward, ever forward, though we do not know forward where,
but wherever it is, compared to our laughter now, it will be
better there.

The former history of former Europe and former Yugoslavia

(Composed on 26 November 2010)

The former Roman Empire had a lot of former Romans,
but fell to former hordes of former Goths and Vandals.
These former Goths and Vandals became then former Christians,
and their former Church had sacraments and sold its former candles.
The former Middle Ages lasted just a thousand years
but suddenly gave way to the former Reformation.
In the meantime, Chris Columbus, in three former ships,
claimed the New World for Spain, another former nation.
The former Habsburg Empire was growing rich and glorious
and former Hohenzollerns held sway in former Prussia,
but of all the lands of Europe which existed in those times
most Orthodox of all was the empire former Russia.
And later, as we know so well, the former Yugoslavs
set up their former kingdom for all their former folk.
And Tito, former President of former Yugoslavia,
died while still the former boss, his country going broke.
Today we know that everything is always former something,
for nothing we discuss has a present name or label
and if you think another way, keep in your former mind,
the former lessons I've related in this former fable.

Humor for the Masses

(Composed on 29 September 2010)

Here at the People's Combine for the Production of Merriment
we make jokes.
Yes comrades -- and we do it for you!
Because, in a people's state,
it is the people who laugh,
while in a capitalistic state,
it is the capitalists who laugh.
So we make jokes for the people,
we poke fun at greedy capitalists
(in foreign countries)
and frenzied exploiters
(also in foreign countries).
We expose the insidious lies
in capitalistic jokes,
and the cryptic messages in imperialist jokes
designed to enslave you.
Yes comrades: we are on your side!
When we make a joke,
only the capitalists and imperialists cringe
and beg for mercy.
We want you to be merry.
That's why
here at the People's Combine for the Production of Merriment
we make jokes.

Ghost comrades in the sky

(Composed on 27 and 29 January 2011; inspired by the song "Ghost Riders in the Sky", written on 5 June 1948 by Stan Jones)

The comrades at the factory were making marzi-PAN,
and talking 'bout how they could best fulfill the Five Year Plan,
when all at once a shout was heard and there were verbal sparks
of genuine excitement at the mention of Karl Marx.

Yippie-yi-yay, yippie-yi-yo
Marzipan comrades work the plan!

Their fingernails were dirty, they were filled with marzi-PAN,
and beads of sweat were building up on each and every man.
They thought about Bukharin and sometimes Stalin too,
and hoped to be the fastest and the most efficient crew.

Yippie-yi-yay, yippie-yi-yo
Marzipan comrades work the plan!

And as the work-day ended, they looked up in the sky
and saw the ghosts of fallen comrades, heard their mournful cry.
They'd failed to meet the targets; just listen as they sigh,
"We've got to work forever in the collective in the sky."

Yippie-yi-yay, yippe-yi-yo
Ghost comrades in the sky!

They'd been accused of sabotage: they'd failed to reach the goal,
they then were liquidated and thrown into a hole.

Their minds had been polluted by anti-party thoughts,
in the act of not believing the party they'd been caught.

Yippie-yi-yay, yippie-yi-yo
Ghost comrades in the sky!

As the comrade-ghosts kept working, they shouted down below,
"Forget the things you've learned in school and what you think you know.
The only thing you need to know is that the party's right,
Remember that forever and keep the plan in sight."

Yippie-yi-yay, yippie-yi-yo
Ghost comrades in the sky!

Three popes are better than one

(In 1378, it developed that there were two popes reigning – one in Avignon, and one in Rome. In 1403, the last Avignon pope fled to Perpignan. Then, in 1409, a conclave was called in Pisa where it was hoped that a new pope could be elected who would replace the other two popes. In the short run, this resulted in there being three popes. This verse may be sung to the tune of "Rudolph the red-nosed reindeer. Composed on 22 May 2011)

Pope Benedict the thirteenth
had his seat in Avignon.
Gregory the twelfth in Rome let
out a very loud guffaw.
Each of the popes would bluster
and claim to be legiti-mate
and call on the other pontiff
to concede and abdicate.
Then in fourteen hundred nine
Pisa's bishops said:
"These two popes should both step down,
we'll choose a new one here instead."
Then there were three popes reigning,
each possessed a shiny throne:
unlike the later pontiffs,
they wouldn't have to reign alone.

Dog food 1968

(According to an unconfirmed story, after the Soviet tanks moved into Czechoslovakia in August 1968, local communists ordered security services to shoot local dogs. Composed on 5 May 2011)

Hey little doggie, don't get shot,
look at the size of the gun he's got.
Quick, take cover, hide your butt,
if you still want to make the cut.

First came the tanks and the marching band,
just swooped in to control our land:
"fraternal assistance" – so they said.
Don't resist or you'll end up dead.
Their music was quite loud enough,
and wasn't Czech but Russian stuff –
plugged our ears, so not to hear;
down at the pub we swigged some beer.

Hey little doggie, don't get shot,
look at the size of the gun he's got.
Quick, take cover, hide your butt,
if you still want to make the cut.

It starts with dog food but progresses
soon to anti-Soviet messes.
Eating dog food from the states?
Dreams of burgers on your plate.
Dumplings, cabbage, what's the diff'
once you've had a little sniff
of those capitalist delights,
you toss and turn and can't sleep nights.

Hey little doggie, don't get shot,
look at the size of the gun he's got.

Quick, take cover, hide your butt,
if you still want to make the cut.

Once you have tasted doggie food
from the states you'll always brood,
whining, howling all day long:
it does no good to bark that song.
Now they've come with guns in hand:
if you're canine, flee the land,
go where people understand
that doggies never should be banned.

Tripoli, August 2011

(Composed on 21 August 2011)

There's no need to worry -- we're still in control,
at least of the city which we can patrol.
OK, not the whole of it, but quite nearly half.
When it comes to the rebels -- well, don't make us laugh!
We still control five city blocks and a shop,
we call on the rebels to surrender and stop.
There's no need to worry, we're still in the city,
we'll send out for pizza -- yes, we're sitting pretty.
We're still in control of the Army Headquarters,
it's only one building, but we have a few mortars.
We're still in control of the fifth floor -- that's right!
and if they come up here, we'll put up a fight.
We still hold the rest room, we'll never come out,
and if they don't leave, then we'll just have to shout.
The rebels can't win -- not now and not ever.
We still have the toilet, we'll stay here forever.

Akademgorodok

(Composed on 16 November 2011)

Academic City – books are us!

We have a drive-in library, you sit inside your car
and read the works of Brezhnev on the giant screen afar.

Our restaurants are popular, the waiters can recite
the items on the menu and serve them through the night.

They also know their Chekhov and Dostoyevsky too
and can recite from memory *War and Peace*, Part Two.

Our research is important, we're hoping to devise
a way to undo global warming: that would be so wise.

We're looking to the future, and want to end all war:
we know you'll be delighted with what we have in store.

Our youngsters – when they go on dates – they take just what they'll need:
and take along some works of science – there's just so much to read.

So, next time you're in Russia and looking for your nook,
come visit us in Akademgorodok and find yourself a book.

Academic City – books are us!

Baldwin XVIII

(Composed on 26-27 December 2011)

Baldwin the 18th was such a persister,
married three women including his sister.
His sister was already wed to their uncle
who presented the newly weds with a carbuncle.
But uncle had two wives already it seems
and one was a man – the Bishop of Riems.
This uncle, whose name was Rodbert of Rhodes,
spent every Saturday reciting quaint odes.
His daughter was wed to the town's parish priest
and it's said that their sexual life never ceased.
But each of the two had a man on the side,
and the priest for his part always tested each bride.
And the parish priest's brother was really none other
than plaything to Rodbert of Rhodes' stepmother.
Locally known as Edwina the Rude,
she often paraded around in the nude.
The bishop approved, since he had a good view,
and rewarded Edwina with her personal pew.
Edwina once slept with the four altar boys --
it's said that they made an incredible noise,
and the boys, at Saint Schnitzler's, once had a fling
with Baldwin the 18th, their landsman and king.

Department of Health Sciences

Here you can study also about unhealthy people.

Lazy mouth syndrome

(Composed on 1 December 2010)

Lazy mouth syndrome can happen to you,
lazy mouth syndrome – there's no cure,
all your muscles lose their tone and flex,
and this can happen to either sex.
Lazy mouth, lazy mouth,
lazy mouth, lazy mouth,
lazy mouth, lazy mouth,
lazy mouth syndrome – there's no cure.

You could (always) try to exercise,
and of course depressurize
your mouth and jaw and both your lips,
but I'll give you a little tip:
Lazy mouth, lazy mouth,
lazy mouth, lazy mouth,
lazy mouth, lazy mouth,
lazy mouth syndrome – there's no cure.

Lazy mouth syndrome I've admitted
isn't something that will get you committed,
but as you slur your syllables,
your sounds are so unfillable.
It's lazy mouth, lazy mouth,
lazy mouth, lazy mouth,
lazy mouth, lazy mouth,
lazy mouth syndrome – there's no cure.

Santa on a diet

(Composed on 22 September 2010)

Santa's famous for his mirth,
but also for his ample girth.
He needs to lose a little weight,
from today -- it's not too late.
His merry elves were once obese
but they didn't feel at peace.
So they found a splendid diet
and now perhaps ole Santa'll try it.

Ho-ho-ho, it's the Yuletide show,
Hee-hee-hee, find a Christmas tree,
Ha-ha-ha, some gifts for ma,
Hey-hey-hey, it's Christmas day!

His reindeer too are really fat --
how did they ever get like that?
They barely manage with the sled,
they huff and puff to get ahead.
That's because -- as is so clear --
they work just one day in the year.
If we had Christmas every day,
the reindeer wouldn't stay that way.

Ho-ho-ho, it's the Yuletide show,
Hee-hee-hee, find a Christmas tree,
Ha-ha-ha, some gifts for pa,
Hey-hey-hey, it's Christmas day!

We Are Gum Disease (if you please)

(Inspired by the song "We are Siamese (if you please)" as featured in Walt Disney's film, Lady and the Tramp, released in 1955)

Both gum tormentors in unison:
We are gum disease if you please (ka-boom-boom-boom)
we are gum disease if you don't please (ka-boom-boom-boom)
we'll destroy your tissue with great ease (ka-boom-boom-boom)
please don't think that this is just a tease (ka-boom-boom-boom)

First tormentor: Do you see that healthy flesh so plump and full?
Second tormentor: Yes, I do.
First tormentor: And what would you like to do with it?
Second tormentor: Let's attack it!

First tormentor: And do you hear what I hear?
Second tormentor: The victim is brushing.
First tormentor: Yes, a futile effort -- we are smarter.
Second tormentor: Indeed, and that is why we say

Both gum tormentors in unison:
We will make your gums turn red and bleeding (ka-boom-boom-boom)
in your gums the germs will be breeding (ka-boom-boom-boom)
We are gum disease if you please (ka-boom-boom-boom)
we are gum disease if you don't please (ka-boom-boom-boom).

Colonoscopy

(Composed on 11 January 2011; the metrical scheme is inspired by "Dixie", a song written by Daniel Decatur Emmett of Mt. Vernon, Ohio, and premiered in New York in September 1859.
It was later much loved in the doomed Confederacy, where it was adopted as the de facto anthem. No disrespect is intended here to the memory of the Confederacy)

When the doctor comes with his big syringe
I wince and whimper and I cringe
and look away, look away, look away at the floor.

He draws some liquid, gives a squirt
and tells me that the jab won't hurt.
I look away, look away, look away at the door.

I don't think I'm a cynic, Hooray! Hooray!
but I don't like it being here,
visiting the clinic.
Away, away, please let me out the doorway!
Away, away, please let me out the doorway!

He's sending something up my anus,
and the pain is tough and heinous,
look away, look away, look away at the floor.

The doctor tells me the pain is nascent
and says that I'm a charming patient,
but look away, look away, look away at the door.

I'm not sure he's a doctor, Hooray! Hooray!
Don't you think we ought to have
someone here to proctor,
to check, to check, to make sure he's a doctor,
Away, away, please let me out the doorway.
Away, away, please let me out the doorway!

Song of the Happy Brain Surgeons

(Composed on 16 September 2010)

We've come to an assessment that you're partly insane,
we're taking out our scalpels and we're fixing your brain.
Just settle back, don't worry, know that you're in good hands,
with every error that we make our knowledge expands.
And when you wake tomorrow you'll feel happy and fresh,
forget about your troubles now and banish all stress.
It's only every now and then that something goes wrong,
and sometimes it's because we are all singing a song.
The other day a patient had an ache in his head,
rather than prescribing pills what we did instead --
lobotomy was what we did, but when it was done,
the patient didn't have complaints and thought it was fun.
We get distracted all the time -- for that there's no cure;
though concentrating's hard, all our intentions are pure.
And if a brain falls on the floor, we know it will bounce,
we like our job, we're having fun, and that is what counts.

The sandman

(Composed on 8 September 2010)

The sandman comes around at night,
how quietly he creeps,
he pours some sand in people's eyes
while everybody sleeps.

And when the morning comes around,
the sun glows fat and bright,
I rub the sand out of my eyes:
a new day's in my sight!

If you can remember

(Composed on 1 January 2011)

Do you experience trouble remembering the beginning of this sentence?
Do you sometimes experience difficulty remembering the names of people you have never met?
Backwards sentences read to try you when confused get you do?
Is life something you have every day?
If you answered "yes" to even one of these questions, and cannot remember all four questions verbatim, then perhaps you need "Big Memory Pill".

It could be that you don't know
that your brain's a little ill,
but you'll remember everything
when you take our little pill.
It could induce some stomach cramps,
diarrhea and dizzy spells,
side effects could include too
imagining the sound of bells.
Tell your doctor if you've had
headaches sometime at some point,
you might also get a rash
and feel some soreness in your joints.
Our pill could also bring on death,
vomiting and open sores,
hallucinations, madness too,
and heavy bleeding from your pores.

Big Memory Pill is not for everyone. Ask your neighbor if it is right for you – if you can remember.

The last of the Molokans

(Composed in Tartu on 20 May 2012)

The last of the Molokans – they're drinking all the milk.
They know that all those vitamins are good for all their ilk.
They're drinking milk at night, they're drinking milk at noon,
they pour a little cocoa in and stir it with a spoon.
They dip a biscuit in it, and swirl it all around,
they drink their milk while standing or while sitting on the ground.
And when they're feeling happy – or so I've heard it said –
they try to drink a round of milk, each standing on his head.

No sex before breakfast

(Composed on 12 June 2012)

No sex before breakfast,
it just isn't done.
And yes, I can see
that you want to have fun.
But I need my bacon,
hash browns and eggs
before I'll be ready
to spread wide my legs.

The Discovery Channel

(Composed on 6-8 December 2012)

You can watch the Discovery Channel, where nothing is false or uncouth.
Whatever you hear on that channel is sure to be only the truth.
A meteor huge and impressive is soaring right in our direction,
it's only a matter of time before it will make a connection.
Bacteria new and infectious are growing and spreading around,
they strike at your neighbors and colleagues, who're smitten, infected, and downed.
The freeways – I've learned on that channel – are full of the most deadly fumes:
inhale them too often and, as you will see, you'll end up in premature tombs.
They've come from their faraway planets, their DNA's blended with ours.
It's only a matter of decades or maybe just minutes and hours,
before they've commanding the planet and civilization is through.
Discovery Channel explains it and so I am certain it's true.
Forks are quite dangerous also – you might get one stuck up your nose:
Discovery Channel reports it, and that is a channel that knows.
Pens that are leaky are likely to drip their ink into your eyes
and ink could be terribly deadly, so beware of an awful surprise.
Carpets when nailed to the floorboards rarely, if ever, will slip,
but if you're not ever so careful, it's possible that you could trip.
For safety's sake we're recommending precautions and, yes, to take care –
You're safest in front of the TV, relax in your favorite chair.

Discovery Channel informs us to treat ourselves with every kindness,
but watching the TV too often results in incipient blindness.
So watch the Discovery Channel, where nothing is false or misleading,
Whatever you hear on that channel is surely well worth your heading.

Thank you for not singing

(Composed on 16 October 2012)

Here in our restaurant, as you can see,
we have two sectionettes where you can be.
Sectionette 1 is for those who would sing
or warble or yodel or some other thing.
Sectionette 2 is what we've reserved
for people convinced that they have deserved
repose and some quiet, a place calm and still,
where they need not join in a choral quadrille.

Is there a wall that divides up the two
sectionettes clearly so nothing gets through?
No, and it's true that the singing will pass
through the air just as easily as light comes through glass.
But second-hand singing should do you no harm,
so we see no reason to sound an alarm.
So, come, take a seat and we'll call the skater
who'll roll to your table to serve as your waiter.

Aldini zap-zap

(Composed on 9 June 2013)

Aldini zap-zap was a scientist of note
who thought human life was electric.
You just apply wires and then a zap-zap
and you get motions quite apoplectic.
He visited England to get a cadaver:
George Foster, just hanged by the noose.
And wires to the body and just flip the switch,
a little zap-zap made him loose.
Aldini then figured zap-zap was the key
to making the dead come to life.
He announced his intention to scientists zap-zap
and you bet the rumors were rife.
But though he contended and though he perpended
he found that the going was tough,
and none of his efforts achieved his design,
'cause zap-zap just wasn't enough.

Department of Economics

"Money is better than poverty, if only for financial reasons."
-- Woody Allen

The taxes, the taxes

(Composed on 5 November 2010; amended on 29 November 2010: the first, second and fifth stanzas may be sung to the tune of "The Bowery," song from Percy Gaunt and Charles H. Hoyt's Broadway play "A trip to Chinatown" (1891); the third stanza may be sung to the tune of Charles K. Harris' "After the Ball" (1891), interpolated into "A trip to Chinatown"; the fourth stanza may be sung to the tune of Harry Dacre's "Daisy Bell," a hit from 1892)

Oh, the night that I struck it rich,
I knew then that I had to ditch
taxes and tax forms that came my way,
better by far that I kept my pay.
I don't want to support our schools
or charities run by a pack of fools,
I don't think I need government –
I'll never pay tax any more.

The taxes, the taxes
they're much too high,
so we'll say goodbye
to the taxes, the taxes,
I'll never pay tax any more.

After we stop all taxes,
after we close up shop,
close all the useless bureaus,
make all the government stop
wasting our precious money –
government off our backs! –
we'll cut all fed'ral funding
and chop away our tax!

Tax man, tax man,
give me your answer do:
I'm half crazy,
we have no need of you!
We won't repair the bridges,
the police will be for hire,

and you'll subscribe to what you need
if your house should catch on fire.
The taxes, the taxes
they're much too high,
so we'll say goodbye
to the taxes, the taxes,
I'll never pay tax any more.

Bean counters

(Composed on 5 January 2011; may be sung to the tune of "Marching through Georgia", a song composed by Henry Clay Work in 1865 to celebrate General William Tecumseh Sherman's march through Georgia the previous year)

Bring along the checklist boys! We'll check the work again,
making sure the workers spare no effort and no pain.
They must use their muscles, but we just use our brain,
as we go checking the workplace.

Hi ho! Hi ho! You'd better not be slow!
Ho hum! Ho hum! You'd better not play dumb!
So we sing the chorus as you try to keep the pace,
as we go checking your workplace.

Sometimes when we point out dirt that's gathered over years,
the workers smile with gratitude and weep some joyful tears.
Then they give us heaps of thanks, while breaking out in cheers,
as we assess what to fine them.

Hi ho! Hi ho! You'd better not be slow!
Ho hum! Ho hum! You'd better not play dumb!
So we sing the chorus as you try to keep the pace,
as we go checking the workplace.

Often we discover that a job assigned to four
could be done by just two men and thus we keep the score:
time to lay off workers and show them out the door,
as we go checking the workplace.

Hurrah! Hurrah! We bring the jubilee!
Hurrah! Hurrah! the work that sets you free!

If you are expendable, you'll be a refugee
from what was where you were working.

Hi ho! Hi ho! You'd better not be slow!
Ho hum! Ho hum! You'd better not play dumb!
So we sing the chorus as you try to keep the pace,
as we go checking
as we go checking
as we go checking the workplace.

The 8-dollar bill

(Composed 2 March 2010)

Has it ever happened that you find you're in a store
and what you want is gonna cost eight dollars sixty-four,
you've got two ones, a five, two twenties, and as well a ten,
you've got three cents, a quarter, and blue-ink ballpoint pen.
You'd like to keep it simple and you don't want lots of change,
you tell the cashier "Keep the ten", she thinks you are deranged.
But here's a good solution that could simplify the sale,
and please don't think that what I want is just another tale.
Eight-dollar note would be just right, Van Buren on the bill,
add 64 cents and your change will be exactly nil.
So why not introduce as well a 64-cent coin,
with Franklin Pierce's handsome face, he's eager now to join
the other faces in your purse, they'll make a lovely choir,
these denominations will bring joy to each and every buyer.

(In America,) the poor exploit the rich

(Inspired by Lewis Black and composed on 25 March 2011)

The poor exploit the rich: just listen, I'll explain.
The rich are most important folk, it's a bother to disdain
the rabble riding buses and making awful scenes
by crowding up the roads which were designed for limousines.

The poor exploit the rich just by their very presence,
they make the rich feel guilty for eating quail and pheasants.
How dare the poor expect insurance firms to cover
hospitals and medicines as if they were their lovers.

The poor exploit the rich, they want the right to strike.
They should be glad to work at all, or if not, take a hike.
They want the public schools to give them education,
but rich folks need their money to expand their corporations.

The poor exploit the rich: you know it isn't fair,
'cause freedom means you've got the right to never ever care.
For in the USA, the poor don't know their place,
they just don't understand at all that they have lost the race.

The rich exploit the poor

(Composed on 25 March 2011)

The rich exploit the poor, but only 'cause they need it.
The poor have hunger for such treatment, and the rich must feed it.
The poor cry out, "Please come, repress us" -- they are quite adroit,
and then they add most feverishly, "Ready, set, exploit!"

The rich exploit the poor: you know they'd rather not.
They're busy with their luxury, content with what they've got.
Like GE in a better year, they pay no tax at all,
they keep their billions to themselves, entitled to their haul.

The rich exploit the poor: someone's gotta do it.
The poor can't do it to themselves -- besides, they're quite unfit.
The poor want lots of services, they want the rich to pay,
the rich don't need those services and tell the poor "Good day!"

The rich exploit the poor -- I'll get right to the point:
it's easy to see how the world would be quite out of joint,
if things were organised to suit the pleasures of the poor.
No, let those goat-herds eat their cake but stay down in the sewer.

Coin master

(Composed on 11 August 2010)

Coin master, coin master, you are in charge,
your knowledge is great, your authority's large.
When coin punchers punch out the coins at the mint,
they're doing their duty but just for a stint.

When punchers punch too slowly,
you detect that they are stalling,
you command them, "Punch much faster":
taking charge – that is your calling.

When punchers' work gets sloppy
and the imprints look quite hazy,
you command them, "Shape up quickly,
we don't like it if you're lazy."

When the punchers slouch while sitting,
and their posture, it declines,
you command them, "Sit up smartly,
heads erect, and straighten spines."

Coin master, coin master, you are in charge,
your knowledge is great, your authority's large.
When coin punchers punch out the coins at the mint,
they're doing their duty but just for a stint.

Amnesia Corporation

(Composed on 28-29 December 2011)

We're just down the road from the penitentiary –
huge yellow building to command your attentionary,
with a giant photo of a beautiful koala:
Welcome to Amnesia in downtown Walla Walla!
We'll overwhelm you with our "isness",
what we produce is none of your business.
Maybe what we do involves steel or cotton,
but what do we've already forgotten.
But if you ever come and seek employment,
we'll guarantee to maximize enjoyment.
Our uniforms are lovely – shirts and blouses white,
with little red bow-ties tied on tight.
Skirts and trousers striped, just the way you'd choose:
that's red and white fluorescent with shiny red shoes.
If you have a shell fish as a little pet,
you can bring it in to work: just mind the etiquette.
We even have a monorail to bring you to your desk,
you'll find our whole facility is very picturesque.
So next time that you find you're looking for some labor,
come to Walla Walla and bring along your neighbor.

Our garbage compactor

(Composed in Tartu, on 21 May 2012)

If tourists won't come to your village or town
that's always a financial factor,
but our town is blessed – you'd almost have guessed –
with a colorful garbage compactor.
It grinds and it whirs, it crushes and stirs,
the whole thing is terribly loud.
But it always attracts a touristic crowd
and it makes us all terribly proud.
So impressed are the tourists that when they go home,
they relate how they're powerfully awed,
and lately our tourists arrive with large sacks,
bringing their trash from abroad.
Now we're erecting a monument here,
right on the main village square
to the compactor's builder, a bright engineer,
who's freed us from worry and care.

Everyone is middle-class

(Composed on 31 August 2012)

There is a country far away with just a middle class,
and that includes the richest folks and military brass.
The homeless too are middle class, the indigent as well:
hell, all of them are middle class, as far as we can tell.
But then one day a candidate for office on a tour
employed that smart four-letter word and spoke about the poor.
The rich folks didn't like this much and soon contrived a plot,
to terminate the candidate – and you know what he got!

Department of Artificial Intelligence

Our classes are taught by robots; we thought they would be cheaper than human professors, but these units are so smart — now they've organized a union and are demanding a salary increase.

Where is my wandering robot now?

(For Francine, Richard, and Danielle)
(Composed on 22 October 2010; may be sung to the tune of "Where is my wandering boy tonight," words & music composed by Robert Lowry, 1877)

Where is my wandering robot now?
Where is my wandering robot now?
Out out out out
Out on a date with the bread.

All the instructions I carefully read
I told the robot to take out the bread
So the robot took the bread out on a date
and they stayed out ever so late.

Where is my wandering robot now?
Where is my wandering robot now?
Out out out out
Out on a date with the bread.

I know a robot's a thing that is grand
though it is clear that it won't understand
orders that are not totally clear
that's why it acted so queer.

Where is my wandering robot now?
Where is my wandering robot now?
Out out out out
Out on a date with the bread.

Next time I tell the 'bot "clean up this place"
I'll take some care that it does not efface
all of the traces of where we have dwelled
and all the memories we've held.
Where is my wandering robot now?

Where is my wandering robot now?
Out out out out
Out on a date with the bread.

Smile, mannequin, smile

(Composed on 13 October 2010)

Yes, hold that nice position
posture very good
great that you can look as if
you're made from timber wood.
But why not crack a smile for me?
spread your lips and grin,
raise your head a little bit,
and show a bit of chin.
Smile, mannequin, smile,
I take your picture now.
Smile, mannequin, smile,
make me gasp a "wow".

You look a little nonchalant
as if you just don't care,
I know you're made of plastic,
but why not comb your hair?
Take a breath for goodness sake,
please don't close your eyes
soon we'll take a dinner break
we'll eat some pizza pies.
Smile, mannequin, smile,
you never raise a brow,
Smile, mannequin, smile,
I take your picture now.

Meeting the challenge of global warming, or How technology can save our forests

(Composed on 31 July/1 August 2010)

Every branch of every tree
really high and even higher
has a sprinkler system fixed
to protect the woods from fire.
If a fire starts to spread
there'll be water all around
and the trees will soon be soaking,
there'll be puddles on the ground.

Every bush and every tree
has a microchip ID
that can relay information
to the forest ranger's station.

For the night when things are dark
we've attached electric lights
to the trees and to the hills,
so the darkness can be bright.
We've installed some rubber pads
on the side of every road
so in case your brakes should fail,
you'll survive the episode.

Every bush and every tree
has a microchip ID
that can relay information
to the forest ranger's station.

'Cause the forest ranger's smart,
he's got switches he can flip,

if the sprinklers aren't enough
he can add a drop or drip.
Let the temperatures go high
to fifty centigrade they soar:
with our high-tech razzle-dazzle
we can deal with that and more.

Every bush and every tree
has a microchip ID
that can relay information
to the forest ranger's station.

So you see that we have met
every challenge that's been set,
we can counter every threat,
so be happy and don't fret!

Department of Home Economics & Transportation

In this department you can learn everything you ever wanted to know about toilets, plus valuable lessons about how to enjoy the TSA procedures, about buying and cleaning your clothes, and even a bit about cooking.

Beware of the toilet

(Composed on 25 February 2011)

Beware of the toilet -- now you've been warned,
you enter my house at your peril.
My toilet's not tame and quite au contraire,
it sometimes is utterly feral.
Just climb through the window or break down the door
and soon you'll be totally wet,
as the toilet explodes, spraying water throughout:
you're soon overcome with regret.
I don't have a dog or a tiger or snake,
I just have a toilet on guard,
but one thing's for sure: you can't kill a toilet,
no matter you try very hard.
You want to break in? Well, just keep in mind,
what the great poet Dante once said,
"All ye who enter should give up all hope",
And be soaked from the hair on your head.
My toilet will sometimes march through the house,
just checking that all is on keel,
and if it should spy you snooping around,
the result will be very surreal.

Dry cleaning with magic beads

(Composed on 10 November 2010)

We don't use chemicals
we don't use soap
we don't use water or
detergent – nope!
We do some dancing
with our magic beads,
and an incantation
that the dry cleaner reads.
We use our powers
the soiling to dispel,
to evoke pure cleanliness
we cast a magic spell.
And then at the end,
dressed in our magic pants,
our cleaning staff
recites some magic chants.
And if you're not satisfied
and still can find a stain,
just bring your garment back
and we'll do it all again.

One size fits all

(Composed on 13 December 2010)

One size fits all, we are telling you truly, we wouldn't be dreaming of perjury
but if you should find that the pants are too tight, just come back and sign up for surgery.
Yes, we can adjust your whole body to fit into the clothes that we sell,
and, in cosmetic surgery on offer here, you'll find that we really excel.
So lie on the gurney, we'll measure your parts and then we will measure the clothes,
we'll slice a bit here, insert implants where needed, and you will soon see how it goes.
By the time you are finished, you'll witness yourself that one-size-fits-all is a fit,
you can shop here with confidence, we are quite sure of that: that's something that you will admit.

Pizza crisis

(Composed on 24 July 2010)

In the telling, in the eating
of a pizza, taste is fleeting
and the taste is best or better
if the cheese is jack or cheddar.

It was a dark and stormy noon,
he ate his pizza with a spoon
tomatoes, mushrooms, onions – fine
but what's this green stuff from the brine?
Origami – now did you say?
with colored paper for your play?
No – I hear it loud and clear –
it's something that won't go with beer.

In the telling, in the eating
of a pizza, taste is fleeting
and the taste is best or better
if the cheese is jack or cheddar.

It was a dark and stormy meal
for it was not the usual deal:
oregano had infiltrated
where all needs had just been sated.
Time for crisis and discussion,
this greenish spice had repercussions,
Down with all these foreign spices!
Welcome to the pizza crisis!

In the telling, in the eating
of a pizza, taste is fleeting

and the taste is best or better
if the cheese is jack or cheddar.

It was a dark and stormy pizza pie –
the kind that makes you groan and sigh,
two little boxes that contained
these greenish flakes of moisture drained,
and parmesan – what's that? – a plot?
What next? Red pepper? Sounds too hot!
In Minnesota, this, our land,
give us liberty and give us bland.

In the telling, in the eating
of a pizza, taste is fleeting
and the taste is best or better
if the cheese is jack or cheddar.

Transportation security

(Composed on 22 October 2010; may be sung to the tune of "Oh my darling Clementine," composed either by Percy Montrose in 1884 or by Barker Bradford, and reportedly based on an earlier song, "Down by the river liv'd a maiden" by H. S. Thompson, 1863)

Oh my darling regulations
I love each and every rule
I will never make exceptions
that is what I learned in school.

When you're on the train to Dallas
through the window do not lean
we have plenty of surveillance
you can bet that you'll be seen.

When you're on the moving walkway
always make sure of your grip.
If you stand quite still and steady
then you'll never fall or trip.

Please remove your belt and jacket
we're concerned you're in cahoots
with the foes of this, our country,
so remove your pants and boots.

In event of troubled air flow
masks with oxy-gen appear
put the mask on as you like it
you can breathe then, have no fear.

Oh my darling regulations
I love each and every rule
I will never make exceptions
that is what I learned in school.

Suspicious

(Composed on 16 March 2011)

I was riding on the train
and a man was talking rain,
when he left he said "good night"
but the sun was shining bright.
Suspicious!

A lady stepped inside
but had trouble to decide
where she'd like to take her seat
or just stand upon her feet.
Suspicious!

Now two carriages behind
it was easy there to find
space to sit or stand -- not far!
So why crowd into my car?
Suspicious!

And the more I thought of that
how a fellow wore his hat
even sitting on the train,
I saw a problem with his brain.
Suspicious!

I shall file a full report,
there's no need that I resort
to falsehoods or to shading:
just the truth, however grating.
Suspicious!

Malcolm on the roller-coaster

(Composed on 16 March 2011)

Malcolm was an all-time boaster, he'd be best just anywhere.
So he rode the roller-coaster, said he'd rise to any dare.
Someone dared him that he'd stand as the car was racing,
from its height down to the land: that was really bracing.
Malcolm said that was so easy, any toad could do it,
didn't feel the least bit queezy, but let others do it first.
The others would not think of it, they didn't want to fall,
and Malcolm too would rather sit than die while "standing tall".
For, of all his many boasts -- this came as no surprise --
his biggest was his claim to be the wisest of the wise.

Naked Airlines

(May be sung to the tune of "Mein lieber Herr," from the film "Cabaret" (1972), music by John Kander. Composed on 31 March 2011)

You've booked with Naked Air,
you know you'll travel bare,
we don't allow your clothes on this airline.

We're gonna strap you down,
so come on smile, don't frown,
and you will find this method is fine.

We also have some first-class seating free for you,
but all the first-class passengers are naked too.
We'll shackle both your hands and both your feet as well,
But you'll see, as we tell, that it's swell.

Each seat's a toilet too,
so if you need the loo,
you'll never have to wait in a queue.

We know your safety counts –
that's why we must announce
that carry-ons don't come on this plane.

You know we are the safest airline you can find,
at last you have an airline where you can unwind.
The stewardess will come and feed you like a child:
so relax, it's so safe, nice and mild, nothing wild,
Naked Air, travel bare.

Caesar salad for the 21st century, or Brutus salad

(Composed on 4 February 2011)

For a fine Caesar salad – I've read in a book –
anchovies always are needed,
but I'd rather have olives and pine nuts instead:
that's how I've always proceeded.

And lettuce Romaine should be laid as a bed,
torn and not cut with a knife,
but I've never liked Romaine or lettuce at all –
I'd rather eat pickles from Fife.

The book says you also need parmesan cheese,
which you've carefully stored in the freezer,
but I'll take some tofu, to eat with my olives
and adding some pickles: Hail Caesar!

Porridge in tins

(Composed on 27—28 May 2011)

Female customer: I want to buy a tin of porridge.

Male attendant: Sorry. We don't sell porridge in tins, only in boxes.

Female customer: No, I want it in a tin. The customer's always right. So, sell me a tin of porridge.

Male attendant: Listen, crazy person, there are no tins of porridge anywhere in the world. You'll have to settle for porridge in a box, or a tin of something else.

Female customer: Porridge should always be sold in a tin,
packing the flavor and keeping it in.
Then you can warm it up right on your stove,
enjoy it for breakfast at home in your cove.
If you don't like it, you throw it away,
horses will eat it and happily bray.
And if you like it, the label you peal
and take to this shop for a good porridge deal.

Male attendant: If there were porridge in tins on the shelf,
I'd surely have seen them, since I am myself
in charge of this shop and everything in it,
so I am the boss and that's how I spin it.
But if you want porridge to feed to your horses,
along with some other delectable courses,
perhaps you can tell me why tins really matter,
or are you so crazy and mad as a hatter?

Female customer: If you won't sell me some porridge in tins,
    you probably won't sell me horses with fins
    to swim in the pond by the lake near the stream,
    though that is the vision I had in a dream.
    But maybe you'll sell me some porridge in sacks,
    your shop clerks can carry them out on their backs
    and bring them to me in my humble abode:
    just watch for the posting, "Beware of the toad!"

Power drill

(Composed on 16 June 2011)

I bought myself a power drill because I want to drill,
but even if I had no plans to drill I'd want it still.
I hold it and caress it, its handle is so fine,
I marvel at my power drill, its intricate design.
I like the way its motor hums: I must capitulate
to hearing drilling really close – there's nothing quite so great.

King of my parking space

(Composed at 5 a.m. in Hundhamaren, 8 September 2012)

Pay attention, here I stand:
I lay claim to all the land
that lies between these painted lines,
this parking space is mine, yes mine.
I do not care much who you are,
here is where I park my car.
So, bow your head and hide your face:
I'm the King of this parking space.
Between these lines I reign supreme:
I've achieved my greatest dream.
When I'm standing in my space,
you say "Your Majesty", know your place.
Here I'm King and wear my crown,
my crimson jacket and ermine gown.
I give commands to one and all,
the parking attendant is at my call.

Department of Music & Dance

If you can sing it, it must be true.

Great Composers retuned

(Composed on 26 September 2010)

Sit in a kavana, drink a spot of coffee,
Ravel wrote his pavana while he chewed a toffee.
Music sometimes calms me, unless it is a warning,
play a little Brahms be-cause it is the morning.
I'm riding my bike-offsky, up and down the street,
listen to Tchaikovsky when I'm not too beat.
Biscuits in the parlor give me such a thrill --
am I hearing Mahler through the window sill?
I never went to dopeland, drugs are not for me,
I get my joy from Copland, I'm feeling glad and free.
Life can be a bundle and can be hazy too,
George Frederick "Happy" Handel serves up a crazy brew.
It never is too early, never too late-oven
to write your own concerto just like that chap Beethoven.
So join the music league, eat donuts from the middle,
remember Edvard Grieg and learn to play the fiddle.

The Vampires' Balle (to 3/4 time)

(Composed on 29 September 2010)

You may be stiff, you may be cold,
but give me your hand and I'll take hold
and we'll dance dance dance
and we'll dance.

How many years has it just been
since you were bitten right under your chin?
and you're dead dead dead
and we'll dance.

I still can recall how it was with me:
one bite on the neck and for eterni-tee
I shall thirst thirst thirst
for some blood.

Mirrors are bad, wood stakes are worse,
blood is what will slake this my thirst.
So let's dance dance dance
so let's dance.

Luminous nose

(Composed on 21 December 2010)

A luminous nose
glows in the dark,
it cries out to me
and sets off a spark.
A waltzing frog
shows elegant poise
and turns into music
all manner of noise.

Concerto for Orchestra, Piano and Musket

(Completed on 30 September 2011)

I went to a concert a fortnight ago because I had fancied some thrills,
and wanted to hear a glissando or two and remark on some musical trills.
The conductor was there and waved his baton and all the musicians obeyed,
and as he kept waving and cheering them on, a great work of music was played:
Concerto for Orchestra, Piano and Musket, with tunes you could readily hum,
and as these symphonists reached a crescendo, much of the audience succumbed
to musings of ecstasy, dreams of retreat, advance and retreat once again,
and right in the scherzo the musket was fired: no one could need it explained.
And as all the audience sighed and sat back, and the fiddlers kept right on stroking
their strings with their bows, the signs started flashing – the words of the prophet: "No smoking"

My pear can sing

(Composed on 28-29 July 2012)

My pear can sing a hootenanny –
something I find quite uncanny.
Did it learn this from our nanny?
for I know that she can sing.

The fruit is such a fine soprano
and can also play the piano,
which it learned at Lake Lugano
or maybe it was in Nanjing.

So I asked our nanny plainly,
was I thinking quite insanely
when I heard the pear mundanely
striking keys and singing odes?

No, she said, it was apparent
that we had a pear with talent
and its singing was so gallant:
we should take it on the road.

Department of Sociology & Military Science

Sociology is the study of society and, therefore, in this department, we study society. Since all of our professors are retired soldiers, we also study the military. We like it that way.

Il Signore Capelli at your service

(Composed on 28 October 2010)

They call me Capelli --
you know it means "hairs" --
we clip away troubles
we clip away cares.
An hour with us
and your hair will be shorter,
it isn't for nothing
they call me the sorter:
I'll help you sort out
which afflictions are grave
and which are the fancies
about which to rave.
We'll give you perspective
we'll give you advice,
all the while cleansing
your scalp of all lice.
You see, we have studied
the wisdom of Freud
and Adler and Jung,
so be pleased, not annoyed
when with every haircut
we gladly dispense
some helpful advisings
for no recompense.
And when you are leaving
and go out the door,
we're sure you'll be back
for haircuts and more.

Weather man

(Composed on 11 December 2010)

Weather man, weather man, you are so wise,
when it comes to the future you open my eyes,
you know about rainfall before it's begun,
you forecast all hurricanes, also the sun.
You must be a prophet, in part or in whole,
or maybe the devil has purchased your soul
and in a fair trade (in a kind of high crime)
has granted you powers as master of time:
you stand in the present but know what's to come,
you are so amazing, it makes my brain numb.
Or maybe it's different and I have a bet,
How you can know what has not happened yet:
you've invented a time machine -- utterly pleasant,
you visit tomorrow, then back to the present,
and thus you are telling us just what you've seen,
having viewed it already from your machine.

In your bow-tie is a mirror

(Composed on 14 February 2011)

In your bow-tie is a mirror,
when I look I see my face.
I'm not sure that for a mirror,
your bow-tie is the proper place.
Frankly, it is quite distracting
when I want to talk with you
that I see my own lips smiling --
what is it you want to do?
What's your purpose, I keep asking:
put the mirror on the shelf.
When I start a conversation,
I don't need to see myself.

Up in Andorra

(Composed on 2 June 2011)

Up in Andorra
there're fauna and flora
and much that's outdoors to do.

Over in China
there's nothing that's finer
than drinking a winer or two.

Guarding Lake Balaton

(Composition started on 30 October and finished on 31 December 2011)

The submarine commander, master of the seas,
was just promoted Monday morn, and is he ever pleased!
His crew consists of pygmies, each less than 4 feet tall:
he couldn't manage taller men, because the sub is small.
He's guarding all Lake Balaton against all hostile fleets –
torpedoes on the ready, the crew are all in heat.
The British navy might invade and try to seize the beach,
but he can sink the lot of them – a lesson he can teach.
And lest the French come sailing across the country's fields,
they'd better keep in mind that this commander never yields.
He's learned to do the tap-dance and even how to waltz
and has been known to tango, but he also has his faults.
The major one is this, you see – his dance is so incisive
that he thinks that that alone suffices as decisive
to hoist him up in every battle as the shining victor,
though if he's pressed he's willing to get a little stricter
and use torpedoes he commands to blast all foes alike,
but actually sheer violence is nothing that he likes.
And so he sails around by day, his periscope at hand,
and worries if the Spanish navy might attempt to land.
So far these threats have always seemed remote and, yes, surreal,
but he's a fierce commander, a man with nerves of steel.

Welcome in our hotel!

(Composed on 17 February 2012)

Welcome in our hotel, guest dearest!
Happiness can be yours
at the flick of the wrist.
Just call our wish-fulfillment table
and reserve your needs.
Breakfast on bed at your pleasure,
wine in your mouth
in our wine-dipping lounge,
and don't forget dinner:
inspired by our chef, now resting.
Have it your way
with our conference center,
equipped fully with microphones
and chairs.
And if you want relaxing
at end of work all day,
a soothing massage waits for you
in the hotel's "soft touch" massage parlor.
Yes, guest dearest, happiness can be yours!
Check-out time is unfortunately noon daily.

Is there a sociologist on board?

(Composed on 24 November 2012; written on board a Delta flight from Detroit to Amsterdam)

In the tower, as you know,
air control can ebb and flow,
arguments can only grow,
with resolution ever slow.
Social questions make them shout,
'til once again the call goes out:
Is there a sociologist on board?

Oh, sociology, don't you cry for me

*(Composed on 23 November 2012;
dedicated to Kristen Ringdal and Al Simkus)*

I read a book the other night when everything was pure,
it might have been Max Weber, though I'm no longer sure.
Or maybe it was Parsons, but I already forgot –
I know I read some socio, I just can't tell you what.

Oh, sociology, don't you cry for me,
'cause I have Emile Durkheim's book sitting on my knee.

Whenever I read Aron, it always drives me wild:
he must have been so brilliant already as a child.
And when I read some Pierre Bourdieu it always makes me cry,
but truly, for the life of me, I really don't know why.

Oh, sociology, don't you cry for me,
'cause I have Emile Durkheim's book sitting on my knee.

Department of Proxy Studies

Our faculty members include some of the finest minds in the world, but, of course, the classes are all taught by proxies.

Marriage by proxy

(Composed on 8 February 2012)

The Baron of Ispwich desired to be wed
to a lady he knew to be foxy,
but the Baron of Ispwich would not leave his bed,
so instead he dispatched a fair proxy.

The people in church were all seated in pews,
many of them arched their brows
when they learned to their shock and their horror as well
that a proxy would pledge to the vows.

"We're gathered together," the pastor began,
"to join in a most holy marriage,
this bride and this proxy, but no, that's not right –
perhaps we should cancel the carriage!?"

"No please, let's proceed," said the bride to the priest,
"I'm sure that the proxy's empowered
to agree on behalf of my real groom-to-be,
who surely is no kind of coward."

"Yes, let it be so," said the proxy in turn,
"and I'm sure that you've already guessed,
that whatever you ask me to give my assent,
my answer will always be yes."

"So do you then, lady, take as your husband
the man who is nowhere in sight,
to have and to hold in sickness and death,
in pestilence, famine, and plight.

"And do you, sir (proxy)," the pastor continued,
"agree that your baron is loyal
to the lady who's ready to join him in bed
and that his good virtue's unsoiled?"

"I agree to it all," said the twosome together –
"the happiest day in his life."
"So if no one objects, it behooves me to say,
I pronounce you now proxy and wife.

"This means as you know, dear proxy, old fellow,
that your honor may now kiss the bride,
but don't feel too married because, as you know,
the groom is somewhere outside."

The groom always pays for the honeymoon costs –
that much is clearly expected,
but the Baron of Ispwich was sleeping throughout:
his honeymoon he had rejected.

So the proxy and bride took a honeymoon ride
to a cruise vessel moored at the coast,
and, as they sailed off to their honeymoon bliss,
raised crystal glasses in toast:

"We're happy the baron will pay for this trip
and buy us a house 'til he's ready
to take on the duties of marriage itself
and feels himself stable and steady."

Now that was some 17 years in the past –
the arrangement has proven quite supple.
The baron's still resting aloft in his bed,
the proxy and bride are the couple.

Smoking by proxy

(Composed on 9/13 February 2012; may be sung to the tune of "Take me home, Country Roads", a 1971 song written by John Denver, Taffy Nivert, and Bill Danoff)

I like smokin'
'til I'm chokin'
but my doctor
told me I should quit it.
Emphysema
cancer could be worse,
if I keep on smokin'
put me in a hearse.
Cigarettes –
nicotine
makes me feel
so serene.
Where're my proxies?
Find my proxies!
Cigarettes,
nicotine.

Fetch my proxies,
have them seated
one on each side:
put me in between.
I've stopped smokin'
except in the latrine.
Cancer of the larynx,
hairy tongue looks mean.
Cigarettes –
nicotine
makes me feel
so serene.
Where're my proxies?

Find my proxies!
Cigarettes,
nicotine.

I think of smokin' every hour every day,
I'm keepin' to my discipline – no cigarettes for me!
And I'm sittin' by my proxies, I know I'm doin' right,
breathin' free, very free.

I like smokin'
'til I'm chokin'
but my doctor
told me I should quit it.
Emphysema
cancer could be worse,
if I keep on smokin'
put me in a hearse.
Cigarettes –
nicotine
makes me feel
so serene.
Where're my proxies?
Find my proxies!
Cigarettes,
nicotine.

Dueling by proxy

(Composed on 8/13 February 2012, after reading a biography of Alexander Hamilton)

Alexander Hamilton agreed to fight a duel
with master marksman Aaron Burr whose aim was sure and cool.
He should have hired a proxy and given him a gun,
and sent him out to give his life defending "number one".

If Hamilton had done it so, as I have advised,
and if his proxy gunman had been properly disguised,
then Aaron Burr had killed a man he didn't then intend,
and Hamilton would not, I'd guess, have met an early end.

So, if you're ever challenged to grab a gun and shoot,
then hire yourself a proxy and promise him some loot –
agree to pay him afterwards, and if he ends up dead,
you're free to go and celebrate 'cause he's the one who's dead.

Exercising by proxy

(Composed on 13 February 2012. May be sung to the tune of "On the Road Again," a song made famous by Willie Nelson)

Gotta exercise,
I just can't wait to get on the scale again,
'cause my proxy's exercising very hard.
I can't wait to get on the scale again.

Gotta exercise,
working muscles that I oughta work,
seeing exercise I'll never have do again
I can't wait to get on the scale again.

Know I'm losing weight,
since my proxy's exercising yes day and night,
he's sweating now,
and he keeps on exercising hard on my behalf, yes my behalf.

This is exercise,
my proxy's working out for (both of) us
and he does it all without the slightest fuss,
and I can't wait to get on the scale again.

Boasting by proxy

(Composed on 18 February 2012)

Boasting and bragging just wouldn't do
but hire a proxy to do it for you.
Your proxy can follow wherever you go
and tell all your friends what you want them to know:
you are the noblest, the smartest, so great,
you're always so punctual, you never come late.
Your deeds and accomplishments are of such note
that people of several continents gloat
whenever they're lucky to listen again
to tales of the wonderful fruit of your brain.
Your fashion is brilliant, you're always so kind
and everyone loves your incredible mind.
You're gorgeous, polite, and – yes – lots of fun,
your humor is dazzling – a thrilling home run.
Your proxy will say all of this and still more
and there can be praises and boasting galore.

Dieting by proxy

(Composed on 25 February 2018)

I'm glad I have a proxy, and you know how that feels --
'cause now I'm on a diet, which means he's skipping meals.
I really need to lose some weight, but don't want to reduce
my daily burger intake, I'm eating like a moose.
But diets mean you shouldn't eat as much as in the past –
So this is where my proxy helps, I hope that he can last.
He's skipping breakfast daily, and also missing dinner,
That's great progress as he's getting so much thinner.
At lunch he gets some yoghurt, but he hasn't so far taken
Anything substantial, much less fries or bacon.
I love my ice cream and my cakes, I also love my cookies,
At just 400 pounds, I think I'm still a "lookie".
I'm glad I have a diet proxy, whom I've wisely guided,
I'm not yet sure how much to lose, I haven't yet decided.

Dental work by proxy

(Composed on 25 February 2018)

When I have a toothache, I really feel the pain
It's something I don't like although at least I have a proxy.
I tell my proxy – him or her, it really doesn't matter –
To pay a visit to my dentist, who dresses kinda foxy.
So he or she, or maybe they, get a fast appointment,
And take their teeth, all 84, to have them cleaned and drilled.
After he or she or they come back to me all smiles,
My teeth feel almost better although it's always I who's billed,
'cause, after all, my proxy goes in at my discretion,
Perhaps my proxy might be thought guilty of depravity,
'cause who on earth would want teeth drilled,
Where there is no cavity.

Department of Marzipan Studies

Ask us about our job placement service.

The marzipan theory of history

(Composed on 12 October 2010)

What if the Byzantines fighting the Turks
had eaten marzipan – would that have saved
the town from the Ottomans on that ill day?
Was that all they lacked, those soldiers so brave?

What if the Titanic's captain had eaten
some marzipan on that unfortunate night?
Would the ship still have struck on the iceberg
and caused so much tragedy and so much fright?

What if the Chinese in building their wall,
ever so high and tightly cemented,
had eaten more marzipan while at their work
and what if the marzipan had been fermented?

What if the builders had eaten some marzipan
while they were seated for lunch at the table?
Would they have managed to learn esperanto
and would they have finished the Tower of Babel?

What if the rebels, in fighting the Yanks,
had eaten more marzipan, that and much more,
would the Confederates have won at Gettysburg?
Would they have beaten the North in the war?

We think that marzipan could be important
explaining why history went as it did,
things might have been otherwise than how they were
if people had eaten it more than they did.

Campaign speech

(Composed on 25 December 2010)

I want to be your president
and if I am elected
please rest content that marzipan
will be what is selected
as staple for each diet
throughout the USA,
'cause marzipan has minerals
and also vitamin K.

If you elect me leader,
I'll do my best to teach
about the good of marzipan
in each and every speech.
And in the U.S. Air Force
our servicemen will get
marzipan with every meal –
all needs will be met!

So if you think you understand
how marzipan can aid
in making your life better
your decision must be made:
'cause I'm your man for marzipan,
and this I will relate:
if I am elected, there'll
be mounds of it on every plate.

A marzipan teddy

(Composed on 24/25 December 2010)

Santa, I know just what I want for Christmas, and I know you
will do your best to find it for me.

I'm really ready for a marzipan teddy
ten foot two and eyes are blue,
smartest marzipan you can find
my ten-foot teddy will be one of a kind.
Hey, marzipan teddy! I'm waiting for you.

Hey, Santa, please, don't be a tease.
I'm in a spin for a marzipan grin.
You can find one extra large,
and bring him down on a river barge.
Hey, marzipan teddy! I'm waiting for you.

I'll take a broom and clean my room,
I'll make some space for teddy's place,
'cause a ten-foot teddy will look great
in my room – please don't be late.
Hey, marzipan teddy! I'm waiting for you.

Santa, your elves, can work by themselves,
but you always try to keep a close eye.
All your work is surreptitious,
but marzipan is so delicious!
Hey, marzipan teddy! I'm waiting for you.

Make marzipan, not war

(Composed on 24/25 December 2010)

We, the undersigned, in recognition of the self-destructive
potential of our present armaments and fully aware of the
futility of war, do hereby commit ourselves to the following
program:

Henceforth all the missiles and guns
will be made of marzipan buns,
aircraft that were once of steel
now will make a marzipan meal.
Marzipan, marzipan, marzipan!
Make marzipan, not war!

Henceforth all our vessels and planes
will be made of marzipan grains.
Instead of fuel, we'll put to use
barrels filled with raspberry juice.
Marzipan, marzipan, marzipan!
Make marzipan, not war!

If in the future Iran and Iraq
decide they want to launch an attack
on each other with marzipan arms,
they'll soon see there's little harm
from marzipan, marzipan, marzipan!
Make marzipan, not war!

Imagine now a naval war:
you can guess what lies in store.
Marzipan ships will melt in the seas,

and raspberry juice will blow in the breeze.
Marzipan, marzipan, marzipan!
Make marzipan, not war!

Imagine fleets of marzipan tanks,
invading someplace: you'll give thanks,
marzipan tanks – why you can eat!
Everyone wins and no one's beat.
Marzipan, marzipan, marzipan!
Make marzipan, not war!

Consider this a modest proposition
that henceforth weapons' real composition
be of marzipan – down to the core!
Everlasting peace and no more war!
Marzipan, marzipan, marzipan!
Make marzipan, not war!

A dream of marzipan

(Composed on 25 December 2010)

If books were made of marzipan
then once we've read the pages
we could sit down and eat them all,
gradually, in stages.
If dumbbells were of marzipan,
instead of stainless steel,
then they'd be easier to lift –
the difference you would feel.
If we took tests on marzipan,
then each and every phrase
would be etched out with care and love
and there would be more A's.
And if our highways 'cross the land
were made of marzipan,
the sweet aroma of our roads
would appeal to every clan.

The Marzipan Platoon

(Composed on 28 February 2011)

We are a rock band – this we disclose –
we're standing before you and ready to pose.
We don't drink the hard stuff, we like macaroon,
you can just call us the Marzipan Platoon.
When we want drugs, chocolate will do,
illegal drugs are not for our crew.
Give us a rule and we always obey,
it's bedtime by 9 and we're "working" all day.
On Sundays we visit the local museum,
or trip out to see the old coliseum.
On Mondays we're reading some novels aloud,
our reading is accurate: of that we're proud.
On Tuesays it's time that we visit the sick,
and when they see us, they get quite a kick.
On Wednesdays we usually go to the zoo,
it's vital to visit the animals too.
On Thursdays we practice, so we don't forget
the music we've written to texts we have set.
On Fridays it's concert time, scheduled at noon,
and so we go down and play a few tunes.
We don't work in evenings, we don't work at night,
we don't work on weekends – we don't think it's right.
So Saturdays come and there's nothing to do,
except to rehearse all the things we've been through,
and chew on some marzipan, if it is handy,
it's tasty to chew and better than candy.

These fish are made of marzipan

(Composed on 4 October 2011)

I'm looking at the fish tank
but the fish don't look so lively.
None of them are swimmingly,
none of them are dively.
Usually I hope to see
one sucking on the glassly,
hiding in the mossy rocks
or amid the grassly.
Their fins don't move, their eyes don't blink:
I think about this hardly,
while eating bread and marmalade
and gulping down some mardly.
"These fish are made of marzipan!"
at last I shout with joyly,
with that I can go back to work
to face my daily toily.

University Placement Service

Yes, you can find a job; if all else fails, you can join the 15,000 happy staff at the University Placement Service.

Now hiring

(Composed on 17 October 2010; revised on 27 October 2010)

Yes we're looking, yes we're looking
for additional staff
yes we mean it, yes we mean it
please don't be making us laugh.

But if you're over forty
you might be a little bit wise
you'll think too much and know too much
and follow us with your eyes.

And if you're over fifty
you've learned an awful lot
you're chocked full of experience
and the training that you've got.

Worse, if you're over sixty
both balanced and mature
you're careful in your judgments,
you are cautious, clear and sure.

But all these traits are vices,
wisdom is no good
no matter your experience,
you should be chopping wood.

No, we'd prefer the careless,
with no experience yet
and those who are unbalanced
are those we want – you bet!

Clarity is not a plus,
confusion – that we like!
Maturity – who needs it?
Experience? Take a hike!

And when our staff turn thirty,
we'll show them out the door
they'll find that they are jobless
and not wanted any more.

Yes we're looking, yes we're looking
for additional staff
yes we mean it, yes we mean it
please don't be making us laugh.

The college of consumer information

(Composed on 20 December 2010)

Here at the college
we know you need knowledge.
Exactly what should we supply?
You are a consumer,
a post-baby-boomer,
and need to know what you should buy.

So every new student
will find it is prudent
to take as her major and choose:

"Best buys of merchandise" –
Sign up, you'll end up wise,
buying what we will produce.

You'll always recall
that to shop at the mall
is the truth and the meaning of life.
So, sign up today
and we'll even pay
your first year's tuition – that's right!

Department of Archeology

In the Department of Archeology, we dig up old stuff. These "courses" were included in previous "catalogues."

There's a rabbit in my brain

(First published in 2010)

Hey doctor doctor doctor
there's a rabbit in my brain
hey doctor doctor doctor
he's driving me insane
hey doctor doctor doctor
he's talking all day long
hey doctor doctor doctor
I think there's something wrong.

Can you give me drugs to fix me up?
(now) that would be so swell
You gotta have a tablet that will work
to get me feelin' well.
Maybe there's a pill that I can take
to shut this rabbit up
He's talkin' lotsa nonsense all the time
I'm ready to give up.

Hey doctor doctor doctor
there's a rabbit in my brain
hey doctor doctor doctor
he's driving me insane
hey doctor doctor doctor
he's talking all day long
hey doctor doctor doctor
I think there's something wrong.

He's chattering away without a break
it's more than I can take,
he offers his opinions constantly –

he makes my whole brain ache.
Can you give me shots to tranquilize
this rabbit in my head?
Maybe if I take some sleeping pills,
the hare will go to bed.

Hey doctor doctor doctor
there's a rabbit in my brain
hey doctor doctor doctor
he's driving me insane
hey doctor doctor doctor
he's talking all day long
hey doctor doctor doctor
I think there's something wrong.

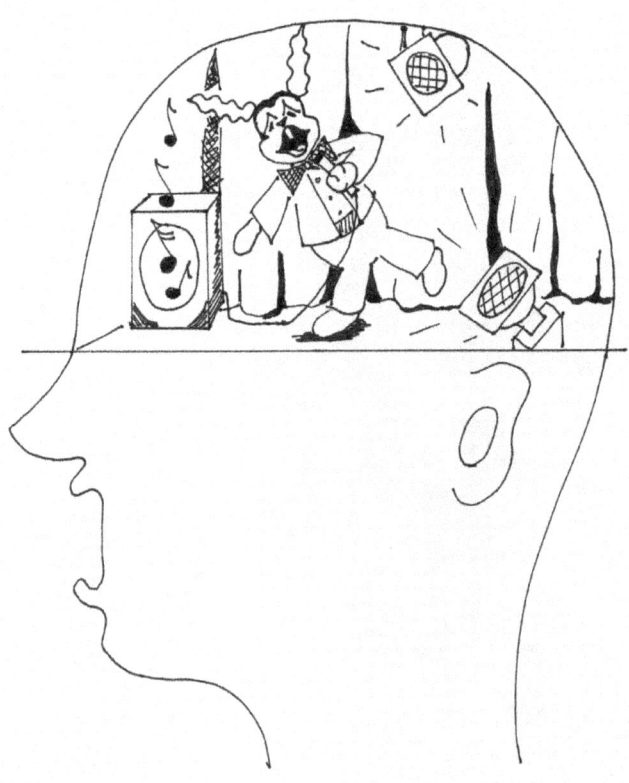

Machiavelli on the Streets of Firenze

(To the tune of "The Streets of Laredo," a traditional song popularized by Johnny Cash and Arlo Guthrie, among others. First published in 2008)

When Machiavelli grew up in Firenze
the land was in turmoil and torn up by war,
rampaging soldiers swept down and sacked Roma.
The Italian people could take it no more.

In Firenze, his city, the Medicis held power
until they were thrown out by a large angry mob,
For Machiavelli this would prove auspicious
The republic soon hired him and gave him a job.

For the next 18 years he would work for his city,
It was a republic – which is what he liked best.
But then the Medicis came back into power,
They snuffed the republic with vengeance and zest.

So Machiavelli was packed off to prison
but he pleaded 'not guilty' and soon was released,
He wanted to find a way back into service
but the man who could help him soon was deceased.

He wrote *The Discourses* and drafted *The Prince*,
He considered that violence was useful at times,
And when politicians kill critics and rivals,
these actions are justified, they are not crimes.

Winning is wonderful, losing is lousy –
So said Machiavelli, who lost in the end.
The Medicis contracted a book from the author
But when they collapsed, he was left without friends.

As I was a-walking the streets of Firenze
I spied Machiavelli or, rather, his ghost.
I asked him what mattered, he said it was power,
Power that mattered to him uppermost.

But Machiavelli is long dead and buried,
In a church in Firenze he rests in his tomb,
But just you imagine him soaring above us,
eating a coconut chick chicka-boom!

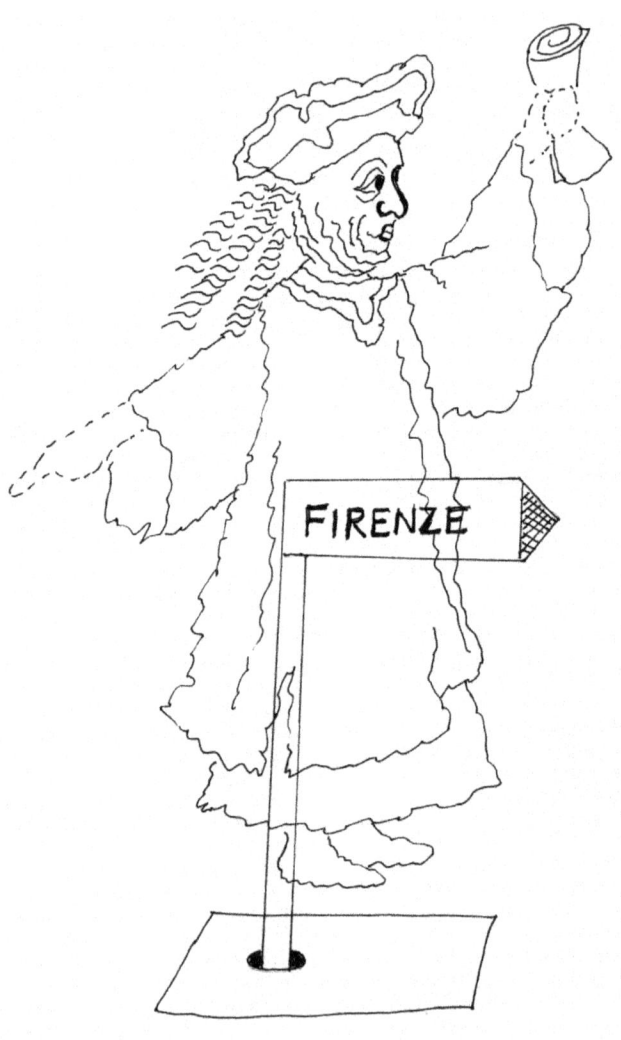

Caligula's Horse

(First published in 2006)

Caligula sat on his horse
and sipped his chug-a-lug rum,
He motioned to his Celtic slave
who rapped his rat-a-tat drum.

Caligula thought he was grand
and rang for his ring-a-ding slaves.
He didn't trust his courtiers, no!
and sent them to toodle-doo graves.

But Caesar thought his horse was smart,
he liked his pitter-pat trot,
He promoted him to consul, yes!
But there was a peek-a-boo plot!

One night he took a perfumed bath
and enjoyed a rub-a-dub soak,
when the barons thinking him insane,
made sure that the big wig croaked.

Tick tack tock

(First published in 2010)

Tick tack tock
Traitors in the dock
Let release the guillotine
Tick tack tock.

Now Robespierre was fair,
But also doctrinaire:
He thought that revolution
Could not be laissez faire.

He thought that Danton's lot
Were mixed up in a plot,
He thought the nation's traitors
Earned the punishment they got.

Tick tack tock
Traitors in the dock
Let release the guillotine
Tick tack tock.

But Marat, he was Swiss
And had diathesis
It meant he had a skin disease
In every orifice.

And every day he read
Another order to behead,
'til he was stabbed while bathing
And was dead dead dead.

Tick tack tock
Traitors in the dock
Let release the guillotine
Tick tack tock.

It shows no disrespect
To do all to protect
The state and all its citizens
From the royal sect.

So sharpen up the blade
We have a renegade
Whose time is up, it's time to chop
So justice is repaid!

Tick tack tock
Traitors in the dock
Let release the guillotine
Tick tack tock.

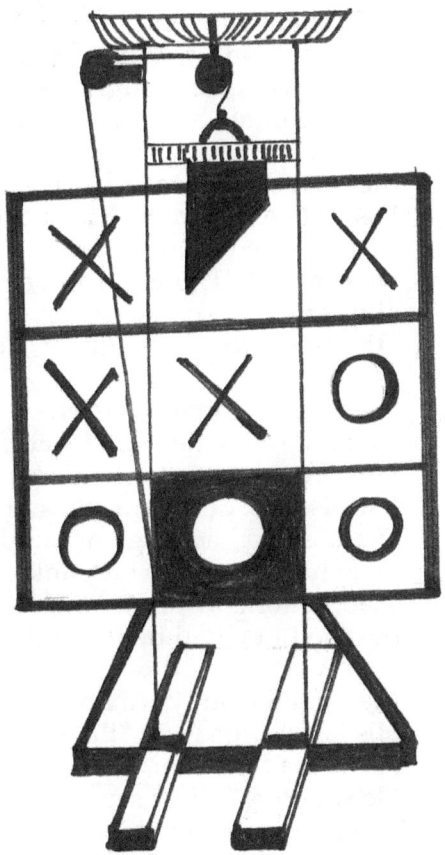

Enver, don't shoot

(First published in 2010)

Enver Hoxha – he knew French,
he had the best seat on the bench.
He knew Shehu from the start,
abolished taxes: that was smart,
built some bunkers 'cross the land,
half a million – that was grand.
All the while he thought he knew
that Mehmet Shehu would be true.

Mehmet Shehu was a hoot!
His last words were "Enver don't shoot!"
As he loaded up his gun,
He shouted "There's just one number one."
"Enver, don't shoot! Enver, don't shoot!"
His last words were "Enver, don't shoot!"

Shehu was prime minister,
some said that he was sinister.
He was tough – now that's for sure,
For his foes, death was the cure.
Skanderbeg had a "giant mind"
or so he revealed to humankind.
Mao Zedong inspired him,
but the Little Red Book – it tired him.

Mehmet Shehu was a hoot!
His last words were "Enver don't shoot!"
As he loaded up his gun,
He shouted "There's just one number one."
"Enver, don't shoot! Enver, don't shoot!"
His last words were "Enver, don't shoot!"

Then they quarreled and they split,
Enver Hoxha threw a fit.
And when he needed a problem solver,
he just reached for his revolver.
"Mehmet Shehu, you've betrayed
the party and it's time you paid
for your independent point of view.
Now it's time to say adieu."

Mehmet Shehu was a hoot!
His last words were "Enver don't shoot!"
As he loaded up his gun,
He shouted "There's just one number one."
"Enver, don't shoot! Enver, don't shoot!"
His last words were "Enver, don't shoot!"

Enver Hoxha had decided
Shehu would be "suicided"
Shehu left a little note,
Said it was an accident and I quote,
"I cleaned my gun and took a breath,
and then it went off and caused my death."
Or maybe it was suicide,
plain and simple: you decide.

Mehmet Shehu was a hoot!
His last words were "Enver don't shoot!"
As he loaded up his gun,
He shouted "There's just one number one."
"Enver, don't shoot! Enver, don't shoot!"
His last words were "Enver, don't shoot!"

Dancing Mind-to-Mind

(May be sung to the tune of Irving Berlin's "Cheek to cheek" (1935). This text first published in 2006, expanded for this edition)

Hegel, I love Hegel
especially when I think I'm so inclined
And I must have sought the happiness I find
When I read *Phenomenology of Mind*.

Hegel, I love Hegel,
especially his *Philosophy of Right*,
'cause it brings me many feelings of delight
as I sit up reading halfway through the night.

Oh the rational has reason
and there's ethics in the state
and you're free when you obey the law,
'cause that's the human fate.

Oh the Absolute is given
in whatever is around:
And there're duties everywhere you look:
at least that's what he found.

Absolute!
I want to contemplate truth,
to cogitate Truth,
it helps to make sense of…

Hegel, I love Hegel,
especially when I think I'm so inclined,
And I must have sought the happiness I find
when I read *Phenomenology of Mind*.

Chorus of the Holy Fathers

(First published in 2006, from the author's opera, "Turmoil in Brindisi")

The Holy Fathers: Buon Giorno! A good day! Buon Giorno!
The sun is leaping in the sky. My, oh my.
The clouds are oozing across the blue. Wouldn't you?
When I saw the pretty lake, I did a double-take.
They say there's trouble in the air: I don't care.
The birds are high – the fish are deep.
I took a peep, and so I know.
The hills are rolling, the bears are strolling.
And elephants are really heavy.
Buon Giorno! It means "good day"!
And a good day it is for feasting well. I feel swell.

The 10 commandments: you shouldn't bend them.
Indulgences, we recommend them.
If I had an indulgence for every saint in heaven
Then, I swear upon my reliquary,
I'd be pleased as punch just like the day
I finished at the seminary.
I swear upon St. Peter's toe, that I'll protect each embryo,
I swear upon St. Thomas' rib, that I will never doubt or fib,
I swear upon St. Andrew's chin, that I'll maintain my discipline,
I swear upon St. Catherine's brows, that I will honor all my vows,
I swear upon St. Mary's waist, that I'll stay celibate and chaste,
I swear upon St. Gertrude's breasts, that I'll be brave with all life's tests,
I swear upon St. Debbie's ass, that I'll never covet any lass,
And I swear upon St. Jimmy's limbs, that I will always sing my hymns.

We don't need life's distractions, we don't need vain abstractions,
what we need is time for prayer and for robust benefactions.
Buon Giorno! It means "good day!" Buon Giorno!

[They all toast and drink]

Bring back my Bonnie to me – zombie version

(First published in 2010; to be sung to the tune of "My Bonnie lies over the ocean," a traditional Scottish folk song)

My Bonnie was buried last Tuesday
her coffin lies under a mound
but some folks can dig up your loved ones
and bring them back out of the ground.

Bring back, bring back, oh bring back my Bonnie to me, to me,
Bring back, bring back, oh bring back my Bonnie to me.

I know that she might be a zombie
her brain will no longer be right,
she's scratchin' away at the coffin,
once out she will look quite a fright.

Bring back, bring back, oh bring back my Bonnie to me, to me,
Bring back, bring back, oh bring back my Bonnie to me.

Oh come on guys, help with the shovel,
please dig away some of the dirt,
my zombie-girl may still be breathing,
I'm sure that she's not yet inert.

Bring back, bring back, oh bring back my Bonnie to me, to me,
Bring back, bring back, oh bring back my Bonnie to me.

Wie einst, Platon-Liebling

(May be sung to the tune of "Lili Marlene" (1938), music by Norbert Schultze. Text first published in 2006, revised and expanded for this edition)

When I'm reading Plato, I can see the truth
All the politicians – they seem so uncouth,
They're living in an ill-lit cave,
they don't know how they should behave,
but Plato, he's my guide
but Plato, he's my guide.

Tom Aquinas wanted people to be good
so that we would do exactly what we should,
He wrote about the Natural Law
'cause knowing what he knew he saw,
Morality seemed given
Morality seemed clear.

Hegel helps us realize, if we are confused,
the problem may be that our brains are barely used.
If every cow looks black to you
it may be darkest night to you,
But Hegel brings the sun out,
but Hegel brings the sun.

Marx and Engels figured, people would arise,
nonetheless the twosome were in for a surprise,
when workers swallowed lots of pain,
in hopes of just a little gain.
The revolution waited,
it was a little late.

Berkeley in a forest heard a crashing noise,
but if he hadn't been there, then come on, girls and boys,

there would have been no noise to hear,
'cause "noise" means that it's loud and clear,
and that means someone's list'ning,
and that means someone's there.

Finally, I'm thinking, on this I will insist:
René Descartes once told us, we think and thus exist.
If we did not exist in time,
we would not think or speak in rhyme.
Thus, those who've not existed,
have neither thought nor sung,
yes, those who've not existed,
have neither thought nor sung.

www.ingramcontent.com/pod-product-compliance
Lightning Source LLC
Chambersburg PA
CBHW031309150426
43191CB00005B/147